About the Author

Namua Rahesha is an experienced shamanic teacher, healer and counsellor. She lives in a small village between the North Yorkshire Moors and the coast with her four children, and numerous animals including goats, dogs, cats, hens, ducks and rabbits.

Her life-long search for purpose and meaning both beyond and within the ordinary has led her through many traditions and to many different teachings. These include different branches of the Vedic tradition, Buddhism, the Western Magical Tradition, both Norse and Celtic mythology and esoteric learning, and Native American traditions. All of this and more is drawn together in her book *The Serpent and the Circle*, which, rather than trying to compare and separate different approaches to humankind's spirituality, looks at the common roots of us all and guides each of us into discovering our own unique spiritual path.

She is at present working on a book for children.

THE SERPENT
& THE CIRCLE

THE SERPENT & THE CIRCLE

A PRACTICAL GUIDE TO
SHAMANISM

Namua Rahesha

PIATKUS

© 1994 Namua Rahesha

First published in 1994 by
Judy Piatkus (Publishers) Ltd
5 Windmill Street, London W1P 1HF

The moral right of the author has been asserted

A catalogue record for this book
is available from the British Library

ISBN 0-7499-1388-6

Edited by Carol Franklin
Designed and illustrated by Zena Flax

Set in 10/13 pt. Janson

Typeset by Wyvern Typesetting Ltd,
Bristol

Printed by Butler and Tanner Ltd,
Frome and London

Through aloneness to all-oneness.
A shamanic path to harmonisation
and realisation.

Contents

Foreword

Among the greatest joys since my own 'discovery' of shamanism has been to observe the spirit of another human being shine forth to touch others with the beauty of his or her own unique individuality and creativity. My reading of Namua's book is one such experience. I had the privilege and responsibility of being a shamanic mentor to Namua on her path of self-discovery. A path that has enabled her to find her own answers to those fundamental questions that have perplexed us all: 'Who am I?' 'Why am I here?' 'What am I here for?' 'How can I make real sense of my life?' In the following pages Namua's personal perceptions and understandings drawn from experiencing for herself the extraordinary whilst living an ordinary life, become a guiding beacon for others also.

Namua indicates in simple terms how we may each experience the joy she has found by extending our own circle of awareness and in so doing explore realities that exist behind the world of appearances. With such a profound experience comes the discovery of an abundance that is within each of us and potential we never knew we had is then ready to be released.

So many books on personal development and esoteric subjects attempt to fill the mind with a profusion of ideas which often serve only to obstruct the dormant inner vision rather than awaken it. This is not the case with *The Serpent and the Circle*. Namua's approach sets the mind free from such conditioning and provides challenges that will start the reader on a path of self-discovery in exciting and meaningful ways.

She draws from her own practical experience in applying shamanic principles that can bring us closer to Nature, even if we live in the heart of a city, and allow us to discover the spirituality within each of us which we can experience in the Here-and-Now of everyday living, wherever we happen to be.

In shamanism it is not a question then of accepting a set of beliefs or metaphysical concepts. You do not need to exercise faith in the existence of realities other than 'ordinary' everyday reality because you can experience them for yourself. This experience is obtained through an extension of the awareness — or what some people call an altered state of consciousness. This is not a hypnotic state, nor is it drug induced. There is no question either of being under the control or influence of someone else. The mind and the freewill are not impaired, and this is a vital principle.

This extension of the awareness into a non-ordinary reality is normally attained sonically whilst being fully relaxed. A drumbeat conveys the awareness from one state of being into another on a wave of sound and returns it to its 'ordinary' state just as surely.

Although such experiences may be extraordinary, they are perfectly natural because we as humans are actually multidimensional beings. We exist and function in other levels of reality in addition to the physical and mental ones we are familiar with, all at the same time and in the same spacial location. These 'journeys' of awareness are means of experiencing these other dimensions of our being. In other words, experiencing the Soul and the Spirit which are our inner realities.

Shamanism is thus concerned with looking *inside* and understanding the essential spirit – the *inner* reality – that exists in Nature and in all living things rather than just seeing and responding to an outward appearance. But most important of all, it is about looking inside *ourselves* and coming to an understanding of our own inner dynamics. By so doing we discover that our individual lives truly do have meaning and purpose. *The Serpent and the Circle* will help you to start out on that journey of discovery.

Kenneth Meadows
July 1994

Kenneth Meadows is an international authority on contemporary shamanism and the author of four books (see Further Reading).

INTRODUCTION

I stood facing the sunrise. I was alone on the shore of what seemed to be a vast lake at dawn. Time passed, and as I waited I gradually became aware that I was not alone. A man and woman were approaching me. Both were naked. As if by mutual agreement they stopped when they reached a certain point. Almost in slow motion the man bent to lift the woman high above his head, then with super-human strength he hurled her towards the sea. She flew over it until it seemed to me, still watching from the shore, that she almost hovered above the water searching for a place to land.

I now became aware of a small turtle swimming towards her. Somehow she landed on it, almost falling, but regaining her balance at the last moment. The turtle was able to support her. As she stood up she seemed to grow, becoming huge, a vast being with her head among the stars, the turtle's back becoming the curve of the earth.

Back on the shore I became aware of something flying towards me. It was a bee. It landed in front of me and I faced it. It was about the size of a horse and I swallowed back my fear. I felt my Teacher's presence, although I could not see him, and was reassured. I found myself on the bee's back as it flew with me back to its hive. As we landed I slid off its back and walked

1

beside it as it led me deep into the hive. I was walking through hexagonal corridors constructed from clean, light wax. Bees, all much bigger than I, clustered around me. My teeth gritted, I followed my guide.

At last we came to a chamber where I recognised the Queen bee. I turned to leave but was arrested by her words.

'Welcome little bee. Leave now in fear and sorrow, or stay in joy and trust, for you too are a bee, a little worker bee. As the true being is the hive and the bees are as the cells of a living body, all serving the hive of which they are a part, so the Earth is your hive, little worker bee. Die alone in the cold or serve the oneness. All the life forms on the Earth are like bees in a hive.'

'Have we no individuality at all then?' I cried, almost angrily.

'Yes, hives when they are ready produce new queens and form new hives. Look back in history and you will see many attempts to produce new queens. But you were not ready. First serve the hive and make the hive strong. All that you learn and gather must be brought back to the hive and shared.

'Study bees. Learn how they dance with infinity. And share your honey, little bee, every single drop.'

Extract from a shamanic journey

This book is my attempt to follow the queen bee's advice, and share the honey I have gathered in order to strengthen and nourish the hive of which I am but a small part.

We are all born with a desperate need to learn. Beyond the immediate demands of physical survival, and social and cultural indoctrination, is this need ever truly fulfilled?

For me the answer to this question has always been an emphatic no! Throughout my childhood and schooling it seemed that the things I was taught were never complete. Intellectual explanations seemed somehow lifeless and disappointing. No teachers or textbooks were ever able to explain the deep feelings of joy and kinship I felt on looking into the eyes of another creature, or the shock waves of horror and fear that I once experienced while helping a friend clear a garden that had run wild. Then there were the dreams that I quickly learnt it was best to forget.

For a while I was able to retreat into a world of myth, legend and story. The gods, giants and heroes seemed to speak to some deep part of me that nothing else in my education could reach. The references to hidden wisdom and secret initiations inspired me most of all.

With physical maturity and the critical mind of a teenager my search began in earnest. As the years passed Christianity, different schools of yoga, Buddhism, Taoism, spiritualism, the Western magical tradition and the teachings of the Native Americans were all explored and learnt from, but somehow nothing completely satisfied my need.

The births of my four children and the necessity of sharing with them what I had come to think of as my spiritual life added a new dimension to my learning. I discovered, however, that none of them were interested in my spirituality – they each had their own. As I looked around at different child care and educational methods I realised that this was a virtually unknown fact!

Now, as I began to learn from my four greatest teachers, I discovered that one of the biggest hindrances to learning is often teaching! Each child was driven by some guidance that seemed to come from within. Free from the constraints of an externally applied 'system' they 'knew' what they had to learn. They needed support and help with this, and acknowledgement and respect for the results, but they definitely didn't want anyone else's answers.

'Of course I was dead before I was born and came alive again,' my two year old informed me. 'But I used to watch you all.'

'People tingle outside their skin; so do plants and animals.'

'Everything comes from the Earth and the Sun, they're like a mother and father.'

All that searching for the answers which my children had somehow been born with! Had I lost so much? Had humankind forgotten what it was and why it was here? I began to seek out the origins of different cultural traditions and religious beliefs, and I began to find hints of a common foundation from which all things had grown. It was at this time I first heard the word shamanism. It is thought to originate from the language of the Tungus people of Siberia, either from 'saman' meaning one who is excited, roused or moved, or from a verb meaning to know. Perhaps 'one whose knowledge comes from a heightened state of awareness' would be a good description. The term has been widely used by anthropologists to describe the medicine man, wise woman, magician, healer or seer of 'primitive' cultures from all over the globe. Somehow I knew this was the key.

Working with that same inner 'knowing' that my children used I was led to a truly great earthly teacher with whom I was fortunate enough to work for a while. I learnt how to undertake shamanic journeys, and for the first time work consciously and deliberately with my higher or spiritual self, and the essence of who and what I truly am.

Things began to happen fast. All I had learnt up until that time somehow gelled. I was able to take an overview of my life and learning to date so that it could form the basis of what I was now discovering. Led by my higher self or inner teacher I was guided around the circle – a concept with which I was already familiar as it formed a part of every philosophy and tradition I had explored. But this time I discovered my own circle and came to feel how it was interlinked with all those other circles.

At last I was shown the true nature of the circle, which is in fact a spiral, or rather a double spiral or helix. I understood the image by which our ancestors had stored this information for us – the snake or serpent, again a concept with which I was already familiar.

During this time something strange began to happen. People began to seek me out. Strangers I met on the beach, in shops, waiting in bus queues, would ask me what it was I did, what it was I knew. From individual teaching and healing, things began to grow and I found myself working with groups and running workshops. I was attempting not to share what I knew, but rather to guide people into finding their own paths and discovering what they 'knew'.

Finally I was given the commission with which I start this book. As time passes I gain more and more insights into the imagery it contains. Very basically the man and woman represents the male and female rays which run through all things. This is explained in Chapter 2. Eastern philosophy uses the terms yin and yang with which most people are likely to be familiar. An incarnation upon the Earth must necessarily be made through only one of these. In many Native American legends the turtle is used to symbolise the Earth. Bee keeping has always been an occupation of priests and initiates, as many cultures consider bees to be the holders of esoteric secrets. I am honoured that some have been shared with me and I offer them freely to you.

The Serpent and the Circle came about as a result of this commission. It was written by direct inspiration from my higher self. My mind simply had the task of interpreting understanding into words.

The reader is taken on a voyage of discovery similar to the one I experienced myself. Shamanism is *not* a religion and is not dependent on faith. Shamans traditionally learn by direct experience and that is the aim of this book. Using the age-old symbol of the serpent you are guided through each level of yourself in order to awaken, heal and harmonise them. You are then led to discover how the pattern found in yourself links to every other being upon the Earth, including the Earth herself, and also to the evolution and purpose of life on Earth, as well as the development of each individual human being.

Having a fuller understanding and experience of just who and what you are you are then instructed in methods of shamanic journeying, and encouraged to explore at first hand the reality behind appearances and so directly access the levels of being previously described.

With this new source of inspiration and learning you are then led around the circle and shown ways of harmonising your-

self with the natural tides of life. Methods of healing both yourself and others are described.

There is no dogma, no right ways or wrong ways, only a few
warnings and much encouragement to find your own path, and
access and harmonise the whole of your being. In this frag-
mented world where we are constantly bombarded with cultural,
religious and political propaganda we need more than ever a
source of truth and wisdom we can be sure of. Each of us has
an abundant source of this within us. If this book achieves its
purpose in freeing even a few of those fountains the world can
only benefit from a shower of truth, wisdom and love.

So who are you? What kind of person reads a book about shamanism? What are you looking for, and will you recognise it when
you find it?

Let me tell you now the answers to a few of these questions.
You are someone nearing the end of your search. What you are
looking for is already a part of you and always has been. It is
that part of you which has guided you here, and now is the time
to learn how to recognise it.

Let us put aside all definitions, all preconceived ideas and
modes of thought. Let us in fact try to move beyond thought to
the part of ourselves that has led us both here to this moment
in time when you, the reader, and I, the writer, meet. Although
we touch initially through the medium of words, let us not attach
too much importance to these. If my name for something and
yours are not quite the same, if I speak of souls when you speak
of spirits, let us laugh at the inadequacy of the system by which
we are trying to communicate.

This book, unlike any other you have read, is not trying to
fill your mind with ideas, but aiming to clear your mind so that
it can take its true place in the complex being that is you and
allow the higher part of you, that is not bound by life and death,
joy and sorrow, appetite, greed or knowledge, to make itself
consciously known to you. This will allow each part of you to
truly integrate into one harmonious and fully realised being.

This cannot be achieved by an afternoon's reading. Nor does it require any adherence to a particular belief system or an externally imposed set of rules or code of practice. It means a vast expansion in your awareness. It means that you experience yourself as the infinite being that you truly are. It means, in fact, that slowly but surely your life must change, rather in the way that an acorn must change to become an oak tree.

This book cannot bring about that change for you. Only you can do that. What it can do, if you are willing to allow it, is to show you how to open the channels through which these changes can take place. Even if you disagree with every idea, every intellectual concept presented in the following pages, as long as you can see them as simply ideas and intellectual concepts, then the underlying truth or reality behind them will still be able to reach you and help bring about the changes necessary for you consciously to find your own reality and touch your own truth.

I suggest that you should read this book through once before attempting to work with it. There is reason and purpose behind the order in which things are presented and it would be advisable to try to work through the tasks in the set sequence rather than haphazardly. If, however, you should feel strongly that a different approach would be right for you then always go with your own inner guidance. Remember it is your own unique path that you tread and no one, however wise or learned, however great a teacher, can know it as well as you do. All anyone else can do is help you to wake up and become aware of what you know, and of course reach out their hand in love and friendship to you, as I do now, in recognition that all paths lead to the same destination, the point at which we are all one.

Chapter 1
THE SERPENT

I am Serpent. Of your myths, of your dreams, of your being and your longing. Feared and desired. KNOW ME!

When you plunge to the darkest depths of life, or aspire to the shining pinnacles of your soul, know it is the Serpent, the Snake that makes this possible.

Tempter, seducer of your myths. Through the openness of woman, the womb of man, I am able to take you from light into darkness, from spirit into matter; for never delude yourself, your nature is dual, you are a being of both worlds, which through me are one. As the Midgard Serpent I make this so. A serpent which swallows his own tail and so holds the world in thrall. Or, perhaps, in the embrace of life.

Through man, who reaches ever outward and upward, I become the Rainbow Serpent through whom you can traverse every colour of the spectrum of your being, until you reach the source, the wholeness, the white light that shines over you, which in reality you are but an aspect of.

Some see me as a tree. A tree upon which your highest aspirations are nailed. Death and life are but two sides of one coin; one must be born in order to die, and die in order to be born.

You fell from light into darkness. Now you travel back to

the light. You too are beings of the rainbow. Every colour exists as a child of light and darkness. All is within you.

You fear me as I show you your true nature. Face me now. I am the Serpent. Know all seven levels of my being. Know them as your own. Never again will you fear anything.

What is the Serpent, Snake or Tree of Life? It appears in so many myths and legends from cultures as far apart as the Australian Aborigines, the Jews, the Norsemen of Northern Europe, the Native Americans and the Vedic traditions of Asia. These cultures appear to have no common links at all – except for one – humankind. All cultures, from whatever part of the world, are created by human beings and their need to understand and live with themselves, their fellow humans and the world around them.

In order to achieve the harmony and understanding that is the spiritual purpose of all cultures, but which can so easily slip into exploitation and domination, the spiritual pioneers, our ancient ancestors, who were able to perceive things in a different way from us today, have drawn many maps to help us. This accounts for the frequent similarities between the holy symbology and ritual of peoples of diverse spiritual beliefs. One of the most outstanding of these is the circle or the encircled cross, but this will be dealt with later.

The first, and most relevant symbol to us today, is the Serpent, for this is a 'map' of ourselves. Whatever our cultural background, religious beliefs or genetic heritage may be, our basic spiritual pattern or make-up is the same. As our physical bodies all conform to a basic pattern, although each of us is a totally unique being, so spiritually there is a basic 'blueprint' to which we all conform. Once this is understood we can all fill in our own personal details to the basic pattern.

It will be helpful if we first consider each 'segment' of the Serpent in turn, before attempting an overall picture. We will work upwards, because this direction is the most relevant to us today. The bottom four levels correspond to the four 'Kingdoms of Life' that we are familiar with; the mineral, plant, animal and human kingdoms. (See diagram opposite.)

Level One

To start with, then, the mineral level of our being is the level at which we are held to or connected with the Earth. By the holding power of the mineral kingdom we are held on the material plane. The strong attraction that matter has for spirit comes from this level. In many ancient cultures the Earth is seen as a beautiful woman who is impregnated by her spiritual husband and all the diverse forms of life upon her are the children of this union. We will see that this is quite an accurate analogy. At this basic level, which allows us to incarnate on the material plane and experience life in a physical body, the Earth truly is our Mother and, as such, through the mineral level of our being, we should begin to cultivate a relationship with her based on gratitude and love.

Although there are traces of many minerals within us it is possible to find a particular stone or crystal which resonates strongly with this level of our being, and so gain a clearer understanding of who and what we are at this basic level. Of course we are not stones, but we have a part of us that corresponds to the function of the rocks and stones of the earth, and to be consciously aware of this enables us to live more effectively and harmoniously on the Earth.

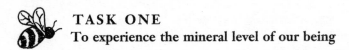

TASK ONE
To experience the mineral level of our being

Your *intention* in this task is to find a stone or crystal that will help you to connect to the mineral level of your being. With this clear intention in your mind, and being convinced of the need for a clearer and firmer connection

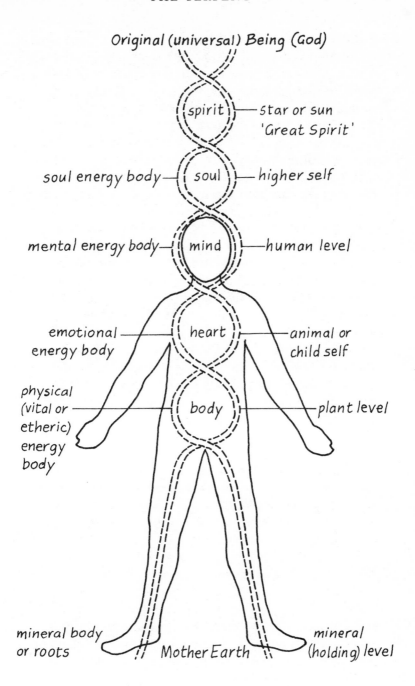

Original (universal) Being (God)

spirit — Star or sun
'Great Spirit'

soul energy body — soul — higher self

mental energy body — mind — human level

emotional energy body — heart — animal or child self

physical (vital or etheric) energy body — body — plant level

mineral body or roots — Mother Earth — mineral (holding) level

11

to this level of your self, take time out from your day-to-day commitments to search for the right stone, rock or crystal. This search may take the form of a walk on a beach, or through heath or woodland, or a shopping trip to shops that sell different mineral samples. You will decide which is right for you. Try not to go with any preconceived ideas about what you are looking for. Put aside anything you may have read or been told about birth stones, the healing powers of different minerals etc. You are searching with the mineral level of your being for the mineral sample that resonates most strongly with your own personal, unique frequency. You will know when you find it. Do not let your other energy bodies, or levels of being, interfere. Act before your mental level has time to question or your animal level has time to feel differently. When you find the right rock, stone or crystal, you will sense its willingness, in fact its desire, to be with you.

A student once searched vainly for several days for a stone and eventually discovered it sitting upon his desk at work, where it had been for many weeks, so much a part of him, so much in tune or in harmony with him, that he had never consciously noticed it. Do not over-complicate things, simply still yourself and you will 'know'.

If you find your stone in a wild setting, such as on a beach, then it is ready to work with at once. If it is given to you by someone else, or you purchase it from a shop, you will need to cleanse it of any negative energy it may have picked up on its journey to you. This can be done by holding it under running water for a few minutes with the clear *intention* in your mind of cleansing it.

Next find yourself a quiet place where you can work undisturbed for a while. This can be in or out of doors. Make whatever preparations you feel are necessary. A good check list for this is cleanse, harmonise and energise. Cleansing can be done by burning a smudge mix.

The smoke should be fanned around both yourself and the area you plan to work in with the clear *intention* of cleansing away any negative energies that could interfere with your work. These should always be directed towards the Earth where they can do no harm. Either dried rosemary or sage make a good basic smudge mix. A rattle is a useful tool for both cleansing and harmonising. The use of both these shamanic tools is explained more fully is Chapter 3 but do not be afraid to experiment, you may well discover secrets of these ancient techniques that nobody today is aware of. As with all shamanic work your *intention* is far more important than your technique. Harmonising both yourself and your surroundings can be done by simply relaxing and stilling yourself. Sitting quietly and comfortably, and concentrating on your breathing pattern can aid you in this.

Modern scientists and ancient sages alike tell us that everything is a form of energy. You will therefore need to be aware of several different techniques for increasing your own energy on whatever level you require. Different traditions, such as yoga and Taoism, teach different methods of doing so, all of which are equally valid. Explore whatever you feel drawn to and choose whichever suits you best. Clarity in your *intention* to energise yourself will count for far more than technique.

A very simple energising meditation is to close your eyes and visualise yourself sitting at the centre of a ball of light. With each deep in-breath your light glows brighter, like a glowing coal when you blow on it. Pause, and then with each out-breath the light radiates out from you, but as the sun is in no way diminished by shining, you are in no way diminished by sharing your light. Pause and repeat until you feel fully energised.

Now you are ready to start working with your stone. Take it in your hands and sit quietly with it. Try to feel it harmonising and blending in with your own energy. Talk to it, either out loud or in your head. Ask it to help you to connect to the mineral level of your being.

When you feel ready, open your eyes and look at your stone. There is a level of your being that resonates strongly with this mineral. What colour is it? What shape? What pictures or patterns do you see in it? Turn it over and examine it from all angles. Perhaps it even has a taste, smell or sound that you are aware of. Take your time and note down all that comes to mind (not ignoring feelings and 'gut' reactions) as you study your stone, all the time holding in your awareness the harmony between it and yourself.

When you have finished read through your notes. In order to make use of the new awareness you have of your mineral level you must bring it through to your mental level, the level on which we normally function, so that these two levels of yourself can work knowingly and harmoniously together.

Perhaps your stone is smooth and rounded, or perhaps it is rough and jagged. Are you a fairly steady, down to earth person, or are you very up and down at times, losing all sense of practicality? You must find your own meaning in shapes, colour and patterns, as I do not want to influence you in any way about your choice of stone. Do not expect to understand everything at once. Most meanings will become clearer with time, and your understanding will deepen and broaden. Take time to be with your stone, and it can heal and strengthen you a great deal at this very basic level of your being.

A student once struggled back to a workshop carrying what was almost a boulder. After she had spent some time quietly with her stone I asked her what had drawn her to it.

'It was so big, and so alone,' she explained tearfully. Gradually I watched her come to terms with the vastness and loneliness of her mineral level. She no longer tried to escape from or deny her bonds to the Earth, and began to work very powerfully on this level of her being. Slowly the pain of her loneliness diminished as she discovered the joy of her new-found closeness to a mother she had not previously even recognised and she learnt to redirect her need for human companionship to a more appropriate level.

Level Two

The plant level of our being is the next step up from the mineral. This level is connected to our physical bodies. As our mineral level holds us in our bodies our plant level relates to the physical functioning of these bodies, in fact our physical energy bodies.

Although your body is made from the substance of earth it is yours to use or abuse throughout your life on earth. It holds within it a genetic memory of your physical antecedents back to the very beginning of life on earth. Much past-life recall is mistakenly tuning in to this level. Each of us is different. You inhabit a unique physical body. How well does it fit you? Do you look in the mirror and recognise yourself, or does the face that looks back at you have very little to do with the 'real' you?

Perhaps you could treat your physical level of being with a little more care and respect. Good natural food and sufficient exercise can make a great difference to your overall health. We are mainly asleep on this level. No one is aware all the time of their heart pumping blood around, their digestive system absorbing nutrients, the oxygen–carbon dioxide exchange taking place in their lungs and the many other quiet, but amazingly efficient functions of their body. Take the time to learn a little about this wonderful vehicle which you inhabit. As you start giving more consideration and thought to your body be aware also of what it has to give you. Why are you inhabiting this unique body? What can life in this particular body (even with its faults) give or teach you that none other could?

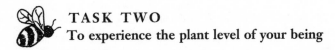

TASK TWO
To experience the plant level of your being

I give two different methods here. Choose whichever you feel happiest with or you could try both.

1 As with your search for a mineral be clear in your *intention* to find a plant that will help you to connect to the plant level of your being. Also be convinced of your need for a deeper and stronger connection with this level of yourself. Put aside the time to take a walk in as wild and natural an area as is possible. Once on your walk try not to have any preconceived ideas about which direction to go in or which path to follow. Allow your body to lead you. Try to *do* rather than to think and feel, as doing is a function of the physical body.

When you find the right plant you will know. Do not let your mind persuade you to choose a plant that you recognise just for the sake of simplicity. Do not allow your feelings to seduce you into choosing a beautiful flower or tall, strong tree just because that is how you would like to see yourself. Try to let your body self, your plant level, guide you to the plant that it most strongly identifies with.

2 You will need a place and time in which you can be alone and undisturbed. This can be indoors or outside. Choose a place in which you feel comfortable and are not surrounded by the trappings of everyday life, which will divert your attention from the task in hand. Make whatever preparations you choose, and then sit comfortably, on the ground if possible, but at least with the soles of your feet in contact with the ground. Close your eyes and try to still your mind. Concentrate on your breath, trying to breathe to a count of four with your out-breath, pausing for a count of four, breathing in for a count of four, holding for a count of four before breathing out again for a count of four. Continue this for a few minutes until you feel relaxed and peaceful, and your mind is still.

Now become aware of your contact with the ground. Feel the Earth holding you to her as a mother holds her child, safe and secure. Allow this downward pressure to become roots that spread down from your body into the Earth. Be aware of these roots in whatever way is right for you, either by inner vision, feeling or simply knowing.

Begin to be aware of some kind of nourishment coming to you from the Earth. Up through your roots and up through your spine, which seems to be the stem of a plant. Perhaps leaves are beginning to spread out-wards from you.

On the crown of your head there is a bud. Slowly this bud opens. Feel the energy of the sun shining down on the petals of this flower and your leaves. Allow this energy to sink right through you, reaching down through your roots back into the Earth. Feel the nourishment of the sap rising through your roots, up through your stem, to the tips of your leaves and petals, and then evaporating in the sunlight.

For a few minutes be aware of this two-way flow. Then gently bring your awareness back to the here and now of your everyday body.

If you recognised the plant that you became, fine, but if not, before doing anything else, make a sketch or write down a description of it.

Once you have found your plant, the next step is to identify it. Books or knowledgeable friends can help if your own botanic knowledge does not stretch far enough. Do not take samples of a plant unless it is common and then only with the plant's consent. Better to take a pho-tograph or make a sketch.

Having identified the plant learn all you can about it. What is the biggest or most beautiful part of it – the flower, leaves, stem or root? How it reproduces can tell you a lot about your own creativity. Is it edible? If so, which part? Is it used medicinally? If so, for what? If your plant can safely be taken internally it will prove to be a very important form of nourishment for you, as well as indicating ways in which you may be able to nourish others. If any part of the plant is poisonous this could well prove a warning to you. Ask yourself why the plant is poisonous, and if the answer is defence, what can you learn about yourself?

One of my own plant helpers is the cherry tree. I have come to understand that in fruiting the cherry gives of itself totally, but when it is eaten by a bird or animal, it has a hard inner core, the cherry stone, which cannot be digested and will pass through the body of whom or whatever the cherry gave itself to and, having retained its own essence and identity, will grow to be another cherry tree. So in my life I try to give of myself willingly, with sweetness, as the cherry does, knowing that I will not lose myself by doing so, but that my own growth and learning depends upon this, as the cherry depends upon those that consume it to spread its seed. This may not remain so for all of my life. As you progress through time and experience, you change and so you may find that after working with one or two plants for a while, you begin to connect more strongly with a different plant and can learn more about yourself from that. Always be open to change!

The main lessons to be learnt from this plant level of ourselves relate to 'doing', or the way we physically approach life. This, though will necessarily affect all other levels, and more awareness and balance here will definitely have a healing and beneficial effect in other areas of your life.

Level Three

As we move upwards, each level is becoming progressively more complex. The third level is that of our animal selves, but is often referred to as the 'child self' or the 'hidden self'. It is what was known to the ancient Kahuna shamans of Hawaii as the Unihipili. (In Hawaiian, 'huna' means the secret or hidden knowledge and 'ka' means practitioner of, or one who works with, thus kahuna can be interpreted as one who works with the hidden knowledge.)

This is the level of all our learnt or programmed responses to life, and also our instinctive base. It is below our thinking level and so is often ignored or overridden by our conscious minds, but as the centre of our emotional bodies it can have a devastating effect on our lives if it is not worked with consciously and harmoniously.

It is important to understand here that love, in the true sense of the word, is not an emotion. It is the highest or most perfect vibrational frequency to which we are able to attune ourselves, and can be experienced on all the different levels of our beings. We most commonly experience this perfect frequency in others through our emotional links with them, but this can be a very unbalanced and painful experience if the other levels of our being are not in harmony. Love is a state of being to aim for. If we can achieve this heightened state of being on all levels we will radiate love to all around us. It is not something to search for in somebody else. Find it in yourself and then share it!

Having understood that, though, what is our relationship with our own emotions and instincts? Do we listen to the child within that is a part of us all? Do we try to work sensitively with our inner child or is that child an uncontrolled tyrant that rules our lives? Alternatively, is that child lost, frightened and alone, with no one to hear or reassure it when it cries?

Task three gives a method for getting in closer touch with this child level of ourselves. In my experience as a shamanic teacher and counsellor most people need a lot of help and healing on this level. Childhood, its meaning and purpose, are explained more fully in Chapter 2, but basically childhood is a process of continuous birth until a complete being is able to incarnate upon the Earth. All too often today it is a process of continuous death or imprisonment of the parts of ourselves which, for some reason, do not 'fit in'. This is partly due to twentieth-century child-rearing techniques which leave all of us with scars and partly due to the society in which we live which tends to ignore, as far as it can, this part of ourselves and our lives, regarding it at best as silly and cute, or at worst as weak and contemptible. A complete adult grows from a complete child. It is not necessary to destroy the child in order for the adult to emerge. We all need to find and heal our inner child in order to be complete.

So be patient with your child as you endeavour to draw closer to it. Give it plenty of reassurance and love, but at the same time the security of a balanced contact with the other levels of yourself, so it does not run riot with your life, nor yet feel lost and alone. It is important to strengthen this level of yourself before attempting to experience the animal or animals tht represent our own particular animal power. This will be dealt with later.

TASK THREE
To make contact with your inner child in order to facilitate health and harmony on this level

You will need a pendulum of some kind (see opposite). Many are now available on the market, some made of wood, some of various crystals. If you feel drawn to one of these, by all means purchase it, but as it is traditional for a shaman to make his or her own tools you may feel that a home-made pendulum would be a nice and simple thing to start with. A piece of wood, particularly from a tree that your plant self feels close to, with a small hole drilled in it, through which a piece of cotton can be threaded, is perfect, but a button hanging on a piece of thread is equally serviceable.

Make a space in your day when you can be undisturbed for a while, and find a place where you feel able

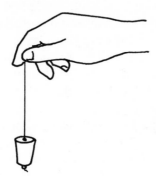

to let go of everyday concerns and relax, concentrating solely on the task in hand. Make whatever preparations you feel are appropriate, and then sit down and relax for a few minutes. Fix firmly in your mind your *intention*, which is to make contact with your own inner child in order to facilitate healing and harmony.

Now take up your pendulum. I suggest using your right hand, as this is your 'doing' hand (unless of course you are left-handed, in which case reverse this) and reach out actively to your inner child. If this feels wrong or uncomfortable, possibly because of other methods that you have been taught, then do what feels right for you. Hold your pendulum loosely so that it hangs about 4 in (10 cm) from your hand, as this is roughly how far your emotional energy body extends out from your physical body. It is probably a good idea to support your elbow in some way so that your hand is totally relaxed.

Now concentrate on that child that is a part of you. Perhaps there is a special name, a childhood nickname, or something that you find within yourself that you can call your child by. When you feel close to your child gently explain that you wish to communicate with it. It doesn't matter whether you speak aloud or within yourself. Ask what the signal is for 'Yes'. Watch your pendulum. Make a note of any movement, but be patient, your child may be a little reluctant or uncertain of this unfamiliar method of communication and you may need to repeat this exercise several times before you start to get any clear results. As well as 'Yes' you can ask for a signal for 'No' and also 'Don't know'. When you have worked out your own personal code the conversation can begin!

Although your questions must needs be limited to those that can be answered with a simple Yes/No/Don't know, there is still much you can learn about this level of yourself. Explore your memory, your emotions and also your animal level of instinctive awareness. As you get used to this form of inner communication, you will soon become aware of much healing taking place, and a deep level of joy and harmony within you that is able to happen through simple recognition of a much neglected part of yourself.

Often, feelings of inadequacy and worthlessness stem from suppression of the inner child. Simply recognising and communicating with this part of yourself can heal a great deal. Consult your child on any important decisions to be made, although you should not allow it to dictate to you. By respecting and understanding this part of yourself you will become a more complete and harmonious being.

Level Four

Perhaps it is a little presumptuous of me to attempt to explain your fourth level to you, for this is the level with which you are most familiar. It is, of course, your human level, your mind, the centre of your mental energy body. It was known to the Kahuna shamans as the Uhani, or mind self. Although not all of us will find that our mental energy body is our strongest energy body we all have our awareness centred in our minds. We all see ourselves and the world around us as we 'think' we see it. This may be totally different from the way our friends and neighbours see things which may be different again from the way things actually are, but, after all, who can say? Even if we can still our minds enough simply to perceive the world around us without prejudice or judgement, most of our senses are 'head-based' and the seat of our awareness is in our heads.

This level of ourselves is our uniquely human level. Although animals have brains they cannot be said to have minds in the same way we have. They are not capable of abstract or analytical thought as we are and their awareness is on a totally different level from our own. This is not to say that animals are in any way inferior to us. They are simply different. In fact many animals may achieve a much higher level of perfection within the arena in which they specialise than humans achieve within their own arena.

You have been learning techniques which have enabled you, to a certain degree, to become more aware of the other levels of your being. You will later be learning a method of moving your awareness from your mind and directly experiencing your other levels, but for the present, perhaps it would help you to stand back a little from your mind, and simply observe yourself and how you work at this human level. There have been many books written, and there are many teachers, both of modern psychology and psychotherapy, and the suddenly popular visualisation techniques, that can help you explore and understand your mental body. These are all quite valid and can be helpful in their own way. We are aiming here, though, at experiencing our mental level as a harmonious part of our total being, and most of the above-mentioned methods treat us as though we are beings hopelessly trapped by our human mind awareness. This is not so, as the following exercise proves.

 TASK FOUR
To experience and understand one's mental level in relation to all other levels of one's being

Go to the special place where you normally do your shamanic work. As stated before, this can be either inside or outside, but must be somewhere where you feel secure, are able to relax and can be certain you will not be disturbed. Perhaps you are beginning to notice that this place is becoming attuned to you or perhaps it is you that is becoming attuned to it. The work you are embarking upon – that of self-healing, harmonising and realisation – is work that is vitally important, not only to yourself, but to the rest of humanity and also the Earth we live upon and the other beings we share her with. So you will find welcome and support in many places. Do not dismiss the idea that the spare bedroom, the garden shed, the woodland glade or the corner in the garden – wherever you choose or have the opportunity to work – welcomes you, and helps and supports you in your endeavours. It is not only possible, it is very probable. You are creating your own place or places of power, as your ancient ancestors did, although admittedly they probably had a far wider choice of venues!

Many of these ancient places of power, where humans have worked in harmony with the rocks, the plants, the beasts and fellow humans towards the greater good and further evolution of all, are now the sites of old churches and ancient monuments. Visit some of these places, it may ease your loneliness. For loneliness is a classic symptom of most people today trapped and isolated on their mental levels.

The Native Americans had a saying that the one thing we all have in common is our loneliness. Culturally we are taught to seek an answer to this loneliness in one another. But ask yourself exactly what it is that you are lonely for. Is it not possible that, trapped on your human level, you are lonely for the missing parts of yourself that you have somehow 'lost along the way'? Examine honestly your relationships with other people, both past and present. Are you searching for things in other people that you should be seeking for within yourself? Are your relationships doomed always to being unsatisfactory in some ways? However deeply you care about someone else they cannot give you what you are seeking, they simply don't have the missing parts of you – you are the only one who can find them. When you achieve balance, harmony and wholeness within yourself, it will radiate out and fill every aspect of your life. But, until then, your outer life cannot help but reflect your inner life, for they are in truth aspects of the same thing.

It may take you several sessions, but try to compile a list of what it is you seek in relationships with your fellow humans. How could the needs be met within yourself? What level of your being would you have to seek them on?

Are you attracted to creative or artistic people? Could this perhaps be due to the suppression of your own creativity? Are you drawn to emotionally cold and reserved people? Could this perhaps be because your own emotions need more balance and control?

Only your mind is capable of analysing the imbalance and deciding to correct it. When my children were small I found myself strangely drawn towards people whom society would label irresponsible drifters. It was not that I wanted to be like them, I was clearly able to see that many of them were as they were because of problems and pain within them. After much deep thought I realised that their inability to form attachments balanced my tendency to weigh myself down by assuming responsibility for far more than I should. Once I understood the problem I worked hard to do the best I could in any given situation and then let go of it. By stopping carrying burdens that really were not mine to take I discovered a new inner freedom that cancelled out my need to seek it in others.

Try to extend the observation of your thoughts into other aspects of your life. Observe your feelings, instincts, physical reactions and connections. Your mind is the seat of your human awareness, but don't let that level of yourself be greedy. Practise observing yourself so that the messages from your other levels are able to get through. As human beings we tend to forget all the other life forms we share this Earth with. Within ourselves we also have the same tendency. Your mind should not be supreme. It has a unique role to play within you, as human beings have a unique place upon the Earth, but it needs to work in balance and harmony with all your other levels.

It is clear to see that as you work towards this end within yourself you are part of a much greater endeavour which involves the whole Earth and all the different levels of beings to whom she is mother.

Level Five

We are now aspiring to understand and in some way become aware of the level above our mind-centred awareness. This is our soul level, the realm of your higher self. This part of you is the sum of all you have ever been and learnt during previous lives upon the Earth. It was known to the Hawaiian Kahuna shamans as the Aumakua, one interpretation of which is the 'eternal parent'. Think of yourself as a ray of life energy sent down from your soul to condense into mental, emotional and physical energy, and be held by our Mother Earth in your present life *for a purpose*. Your soul level is not another aspect of you, *you are an aspect of your soul*.

When working with the lower levels of yourself you have been attempting to be aware of what is within you. When reaching up to your soul level you are attempting to expand your awareness to touch something far vaster, greater and wiser than your human self. It is not a part of you, but something that you are a part of.

You could think of your soul as your true self. When you were a child you knew that you were growing bigger all the time.

As an adult you are still not fully grown. You have only grown to your fourth (human) level. As the serpent diagram shows you have still to reach the fifth level of yourself. This level is none the less still there and waiting. You may experience flashes of inspiration and understanding as your higher self is able to reach down and touch your mind self. You may also experience the odd feeling of rising above yourself, or looking down on yourself, as reported in many near death experiences, when your awareness is able to rise up to your soul level for a brief time, as it will do when your other energy bodies fall away on your death.

 TASK FIVE
To become aware of one's fifth or soul level

Sit comfortably in your special place. Try to have some part of your body in contact with the ground, either the soles of your feet or the base of your spine. Now close your eyes and try to still your mind. Concentrating on your breath may aid you in this. Try to breathe rhythmically. Use a 4-4-4-4 pattern, i.e. breathe out to the count of four, rest for a count of four, breath in to the count of four and then hold for a count of four. Repeat. This will bring you in harmony with this fourth world in which we live. If this does not feel comfortable then experiment until you find a pattern that feels right for you.

When you feel totally relaxed and detached from your everyday thoughts and worries, try to become aware of your contact with the ground. Even if you are in an upstairs room be aware of the part of your body that is in contact with the floor – your closest connection to the Earth. Feel the power of the Earth pulling you down to her, holding you safe and secure as a mother lovingly holds her child. Feel roots reaching down from the base of your spine, being drawn down deep into the Earth. For a while be aware only of this downward pull . . .

Now gradually become aware not only of the pull downwards, but also of a force that seems to rise upwards from the Earth, through your roots and into your body. This is a power that the Earth is giving to you. Feel the power fill your body and, as you do so, become aware of your body . . . the position you are sitting in . . . any areas of tension or discomfort. Be aware of your lungs as they rhythmically take in and expel air. Be aware of the rhythmic beating of your heart and the pulsing of your blood. Try to feel how the core of your physical being, your skeleton, fits together deep inside you. If you become aware of any areas of tension or dis-ease, try to ease them. Move if necessary.

Now let your body fade away from your awareness. Become aware instead of your feelings. Are you happy or sad? Confident or nervous? Are your emotions seated firmly within you or are you being pulled 'off-balance' by someone or something else? If this is so, try now to loosen the hold and align your emotional body so that it is centred correctly within you. For a few moments just try to be aware of your feelings and emotions without becoming involved in them. Simply observe.

Now move your awareness up a step to your mind. Let your thoughts drift across your mind without trying to stop them. Simply be aware of them. Perhaps you are able to observe the main direction of your thoughts. Are they mostly abstract or closely bound up with another level of your being? Are you thinking of your body and how to meet its needs? Or are your thoughts mainly about your emotional life? Simply observe and learn about yourself.

Now move your awareness up a little higher. Become aware of a bright white light, like a small sun, that is just above your head. Do not try to imagine this light, simply let your awareness expand or rise enough to encompass it. For you are not entering the realms of fantasy, you are endeavouring to become aware of a part of you that is normally out of, or beyond the scope of, your normal conscious awareness.

As you begin to feel, or see, or experience in whatever way is right for you, the centre of your soul body, feel the light from it shining down over you. Feel the light penetrating your mind. Make a note of any sudden illuminating or enlightening thoughts that come with it.

Allow the light to shine down around you and through you until it penetrates your heart. How does it make you feel? Be aware of any new feelings or emotions.

Now the light is shining right through your body. Perhaps it has a sound? A taste? Make a note of any sensation it brings with it as it penetrates every level of your being and now, through you, reaches down into the Earth.

For a few moments simply bathe in this healing light. Know that this is part of your being. This wonderful, healing, joyful, illuminating light comes from a level of yourself that you are normally cut off from. Resolve never to forget this level of yourself again and to allow the light of your soul to shine into every part of your life.

When you are ready let all of this slowly fade away from your awareness as it contracts back to the here and now of your everyday life.

Open your eyes, take a few deep breaths and stretch. I suggest that you do not plunge straight back into your day, but take the time to earth yourself properly by either having something to eat and drink or doing a few physical exercises.

The first time that this soul awareness exercise is performed can be a wonderful experience. I suggest, however, that it should become a regular self-healing and energising part of your life. Performed about once a week I am sure that you will soon feel the difference that it makes to you.

Levels Six and Seven

Your spiritual source, or the animating force from which your being springs, is not personal to you. It is, rather, a Father which you have in common with all the beings on the Earth. The physical manifestation of your spiritual source is the sun.

In order to explain this sixth level, however, it is necessary to speak also of the seventh level which can be considered as the Totality of All Things. Although words – a tool of our fourth level – are really totally inadequate to convey such concepts, names that have been used to describe this level are God, Heaven, Nirvana, Universal Being, Cosmic Consciousness etc.

This seventh, God level of ourselves and all things is obviously infinite, and encompasses everything else we have discussed. This level, however, is a state of pure Being, not doing, and in order to learn, grow and change, and evolve it is necessary for God (for want of a better word) to condense itself into Spirit which is the highest form of energy. On the levels at which our awareness resides we perceive these spots where the infinite has condensed itself into a form of energy, as stars. Therefore our own sun is truly our Father in that it is the spiritual source of us all, as well as the energy source that maintains all life on Earth.

We can think of ourselves as rays of light, pure spirit light, all springing from the same source. As each light ray becomes separate from all others it becomes condensed into a more dense form of energy – soul energy. This then condenses down still further to mental energy, then to emotional energy, to physical energy, and finally to matter, the substance of the Earth, a level at which we all again meet, although on the shamanic web we will discover that all other levels are also interconnected.

It is not really possible to give any exercises which can expand your awareness to spirit (sixth) level or beyond. Your path to spirit consciousness is through your soul or fifth level. As you become more aware on this level, as working through the exercises in this book will aid you in doing, you will find the teaching or guidance necessary for your own individual development given to you on this fifth level. No book can really do more than point the way beyond the fourth world, as, by its very nature, it is limited to the fourth level.

Energy Centres and Energy Bodies

Working through the first part of this chapter and having now experienced, and to some degree understood, how the seven levels of the Serpent relate to you personally, you will, no doubt, have begun to see how this links in with many teachings, philosophies or schools of thought that you may previously have come into contact with. From the diagram on page 32 it can be seen that the Vedic teachings of Ancient India about chakra or energy centres, with which many people will be familiar, are actually a portion of the Serpent. Perhaps it would be helpful, before going any further, to examine what light your new understanding may shed upon this ancient wisdom. By linking the colours of these centres, or gateways, with the picture we have already built up, we may also begin to glimpse the Rainbow Serpent of the Australian Aborigines, or Bifrost the ancient Nordic Rainbow Bridge, both of which were understood to link Heaven and Earth, or the spiritual and material planes.

In Vedic traditions humanity's link with the darkness below, or our mineral level, was often denied (the reasons for this will be discussed in Chapter 2), so this was not incorporated into their spiritual picture of human beings.

BASE CHAKRA

We shall begin, then, by considering the base, or root chakra, which is located at the base of the spine, and the colour of which is red. From the diagram it will be clear that this is not actually an energy centre, but rather a cross-over point, or gateway between the mineral level, or our connection with the Earth, and the physical energy centre. If it is too tightly closed we may

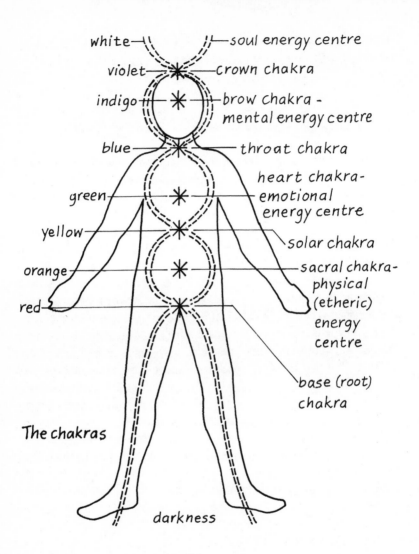

white — soul energy centre

violet — crown chakra

indigo — brow chakra - mental energy centre

blue — throat chakra

green — heart chakra - emotional energy centre

yellow — solar chakra

orange — sacral chakra - physical (etheric) energy centre

red — base (root) chakra

The chakras

darkness

not be firmly enough linked to the Earth. This can lead to us denying a large part of ourselves and is often a problem of those who believe that in order to achieve true spirituality they must first repudiate their physical bodies. It can also manifest itself as an inability to connect with the consequences of our actions and therefore take responsibility for them. If this energy gateway is too widely open, or slack, however, it is possible to become so firmly set in our ways that we become almost inert. It can also result in a collector/hoarder type personality.

SACRAL CHAKRA

The second or sacral chakra is situated a little below the navel and is associated with the colour orange. It is the centre of our physical energy body, often called the etheric or vital body. This extends about 1 in (2.5 cm) out from our physical body and can often be quite easily seen or felt by those just beginning to develop their psychic abilities. If you have never attempted this kind of perception before, now would be a good time to try. It helps to have a cooperative partner to practise on, but if no one is available try at least to feel your own etheric body by holding your left hand about 1 in (2.5 cm) or so away from the skin of any part of your body, and moving it gently up and down until you become aware of some kind of resistance. You may at first confuse this with simple body heat, but with practice it will become clear that you are experiencing a definite energy boundary. Some people feel a type of warmth, others coolness and still others a kind of tingling, and we all interpret what we experience according to our own individual sensory vocabulary. As in previous work, before starting, be quite clear in your intention to perceive your (or your friend's) physical energy body (see diagram on page 34).

If you have a cooperative friend it is easier to see different energy bodies in darkness, or semi-darkness. If your partner stands against a plain white wall try not to stare at them, but rather let your eyes relax as though you were looking past them into the distance. It will be best to remove any sight-aids you normally wear, as these limit your vision to the purely physically accepted norm. In fact many sight defects are not actually defects at all, but simply a different type of sight from that which is considered 'normal'. You should start to become aware of a faint light extending about 1 in (2.5 cm) or so out from your friend's body. Perhaps you will be able to put a colour to this, if not that

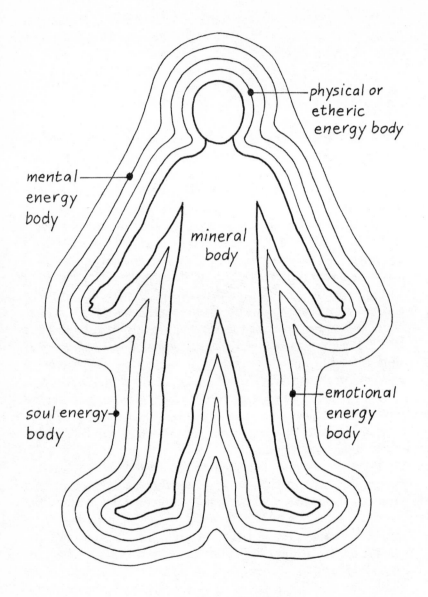

physical or
etheric
energy body

mental
energy
body

mineral
body

emotional
energy
body

soul energy-
body

The energy bodies

will come later. It is also possible to do this exercise with a house plant or animal, but I find the best initial results are obtained with human beings.

As you have already experienced, this physical energy level is our plant level and is mainly concerned with your physical body and its functioning. It is your 'doing' energy and, as such, has been active from your birth for your growth, digestion and movement. It is traditionally thought to be the chakra mainly involved with reproduction, but this is not strictly true. It is the energy centre through which the physical energy required by the growing body of a child in the womb is channelled, but as you have already experienced a human being is made up of far more than just a physical body and so all the energy centres of a pregnant woman are involved in the process of building up a complete vehicle for an incarnating soul to inhabit and develop.

SOLAR PLEXUS CHAKRA

Moving up to the solar plexus chakra, which is situated between the twelfth thoracic vertebra and the first lumbar vertebra of the spine, or a little above the navel and just below the ribs, and the colour of which is yellow, it will be seen again that this is not an energy centre, but a gateway between your physical energy centre and your emotional energy centre. If you find that your life is ruled by other people's emotions or that the actions of others cause you undue emotional anguish, then it is likely that you are too open to outside influence on this level. If, however, you find it difficult to express your emotions physically or your physical relationships are devoid of any real feelings, then this chakra is probably too tightly shut.

This energy gateway is also the level through which what is sometimes called astral or soul travel takes place. This is quite a different thing from shamanic journeying which, as a function of the fifth or soul level of ourselves, is not restricted to working on any particular level. Indeed, the experienced shaman is able to reach out with his or her higher self to heal or balance on whatever level is required, whereas the astral traveller is limited to the level on which he or she leaves the body. This will be explained in more depth in Chapter 3, although no methods are given which will take us out of our own energy system. It is often reported by those who have experienced astral travel that while they are 'out of their bodies' a gold thread binds them to the solar plexus of their physical body, which is usually sleeping or in trance when this takes place. What actually happens is that in effect the solar gateway is stretched so that all of our other energy bodies are able to move away from the physical body and spend some time on the 'astral plane' which exists at this level between the physical and below the emotional. It will be obvious that this is not a particularly high level. It is important to realise that all 'out of body experiences' and disincarnate beings are not necessarily of a very high spiritual order. All have their place within the order of things, but do not be fooled into pursuing something that is less than what you already have, simply because it is different. It is possible to run into difficulties on the astral plane where you will be out of phase with your own life energy stream. It is the level of what are sometimes called earthbound spirits, human beings who, after physical death, have too many attachments to let go of their other energy bodies. Some mediums and shamans engage in rescue work on this level, but I cannot emphasise strongly enough that the astral plane is not the place for idle exploration. We are endeavouring to harmonise all the different levels of our beings, not disjoint them further.

HEART CHAKRA

Moving up once more we come to the heart chakra, the colour of which is green and which is the centre of your emotional energy body. This extends out about 4 to 6 in (10 to 15 cm) from your physical body, but is a little more difficult to perceive than your etheric body as it is made up of a finer and more diffuse energy. Using the same methods as before it may take a little more practice until it can be seen or felt clearly. This is the centre of your animal or child level and as such should be a source of the kind of strength that comes from the openness and trust that is possible when one is in perfect balance and harmony within oneself, for fear is something that comes from within.

THROAT CHAKRA

The next chakra we come to, located in the region of the throat, is the gateway between the emotional energy centre and the mental energy centre. Its colour is blue. When our thoughts are dominated by emotions, either our own or other people's, or when cold, hard logic inhibits us emotionally, or our emotions are subject to the mental energy of others, then this gateway is too open. When our minds and emotions seem totally at odds, then this gateway is too tightly closed and there is no room for a harmonious flow of energies to take place between these two levels. All the gateway chakras are connected with communication, but this one most of all, as it is by way of this gate that our mentally aware human selves reach out to others through the medium of speech.

BROW CHAKRA

We move next to the sixth chakra which is situated on the brow, just above the bridge of the nose, in the area that is sometimes referred to as the third eye. Its colour is indigo, a bluish purple, and it is the centre of our mental energy bodies, the level at which our human awareness resides. The actual mental energy body extends about 10 in (25 cm) out from our physical bodies. Mental energy, though, being even more diffuse than emotional energy may take a little more practice to perceive.

CROWN CHAKRA

Finally we come to the crown chakra, situated on the top of the head in the place where a new-born baby has a soft spot. Its colour is violet, and it is the gateway between the mental body and the soul body. This is a gateway which, in most people, is firmly closed, and which must be opened if we are to work in harmony and cooperation with our soul energy or higher self. The directions given in Task five will help with this, as will the exercise given at the end of this chapter.

The centre of the soul body is not usually seen as a chakra for reasons which will be explained in the next chapter, but it is situated just over your head. If you reach your arms up over your head and curve them around until your fingertips just touch it, you will be encompassing your soul energy centre, although your actual soul energy body extends out about 12 to 15 in (30 to 38 cm) from your physical body, encompassing it in an egg-shaped cocoon of energy. With enough practice this, too, can be perceived by whichever method comes easiest to you.

soul energy
centre

The colour of your soul energy centre is white. Perhaps now it is possible to see how the full spectrum is arrayed in us all, between the darkness of the Earth and the white light of our souls creating a rainbow bridge within each one of us linking our material and spiritual natures.

Just as colour is a property of light, and the colour of an object is simply the part of the spectrum that it is able to reflect, not a property of its own, so the colour of each of your energy centres shows which part of your full spiritual spectrum works through each, from the white light of your soul, which encompasses the full spectrum, through each colour of the rainbow. This opens the doors to an understanding of how colour healing is able to work and to discovering the true nature of colour within yourself.

 ## RAINBOW BREATH

The above description is that of a human being in perfect balance and harmony. Alas, this is a rather rare state of affairs. We can all benefit from regularly working to harmonise and balance the flow and exchange of energy between the chakras. This can be done by means of an exercise that uses colour.

Make sure before attempting this exercise that you are quite certain of the locations and colours of each of the chakras.

Sitting comfortably in your special place, relax and prepare yourself to work. When you are ready to begin close your eyes and concentrate on your breath. While your lungs are empty be aware of the immense power of the Earth beneath you, power that is yours to call on by right of your birth here on the Earth. As you breathe in count slowly to seven and, as you do so, consciously draw the power of your Mother Earth up through each of your chakras in turn, attempting to light each up with its own colour using the power you are drawing through it. As you emerge from your crown chakra hold your breath for a moment while the power you have drawn up floods into your soul energy centre, then with a gasp release your breath through your mouth, at the same time feeling the white light of your soul pour down through and around you into the Earth. Repeat this as many times as you wish.

Having now explored how the Serpent relates to us personally it is time to look outward and discover how it is also a pattern of evolution and development on a much larger scale. We must not lose sight, however, of our own unique parts in this whole.

Chapter 2
EVOLUTION

Long before this world existed there was another world, the first world far below where we are now.

Begochiddy, the child of the sun, who was neither man nor woman, made four mountains in that world. One to the east, one to the south, one to the west and one to the north. Many stories are told of the first world but all we really know is that things weren't right.

Begochiddy instructed First Man to gather together all the things of the first world, then all of the people gathered together on the vast mountain that Begochiddy had created in the centre of that world. There Begochiddy planted the Big Reed and as it grew the people were able to climb up its hollow centre until they reached the second world.

In the second world Begochiddy created plants. For a while everyone was happy, but then again things began to go wrong. Again Begochiddy planted the Big Reed and instructed First Man and the others to put all the things of the second world into it, and as it grew it carried them all to the third world.

In this world Begochiddy made water, birds and animals, trees and lightning. Although there was no sun there was light. At first all went well, but after a while the people began to quarrel among themselves, and this let illness and disease into the world. Finally Begochiddy warned them that if there was any more trouble the third world would be destroyed by a flood. Soon the waters began to rise but Begochiddy took pity on the people and again planted Big Reed. But this time Big Reed stopped growing before it reached the fourth world. Begochiddy managed to climb up and found there were other powerful beings in this world. With their help he prepared it for his people, but still they were not able to rise to it.

Begochiddy started to search. Finally he found, hidden in the folds of Coyote's cloak, a water baby. Begochiddy forced Coyote to return the water child to its rightful place in the third world, and so at last the Big Reed grew and the people were able to go out into the fourth world, where they are living to this day.

A Navajo Story of Creation

We have only discussed, as yet, the different segments of the Serpent and how they relate to us. It can be seen from the Serpent illustration that the great serpent is actually formed from the bodies of two other snakes. These can be considered as the male and female sides of our natures or, according to the Taoist tradition, the yin (female) and yang (male) aspects of which all things are composed.

As you worked through the first chapter, gradually experiencing each level of your being in a totally new way, it probably became clear to you that, whereas your material nature is in no way a fixed or permanent thing, on the higher levels your soul, or spiritual nature, although hopefully learning and growing all the time, has qualities of constancy that are not to be found in other aspects of your being. Spirit or soul is seen in all traditions as being 'eternal' – that is without beginning or end. Taking this understanding a step further it can be seen that our existence as spiritual beings must necessarily have preceded our descent (or fall) into matter.

In very ancient cultures, such as most Vedic traditions and

the Jewish Old Testament myths, our transition from the spiritual realms to our present earthly lives was felt to be a kind of punishment or banishment. This is not strictly true, since taking a spiritual view of evolution as explained in this chapter, humanity's incarnation on the material plane, however painful and difficult it may seem at times, is absolutely necessary in order for humanity to develop according to its true nature. As we have already experienced, while working through the chakras with the rainbow bridge, we are beings whose true nature can be seen as a bridge between all levels. Our ancient ancestors, though, in whom this bridge was still being built up, experienced their spiritual natures as far more real than their physical existence – just the reverse of us today. They therefore felt that all time spent on the material plane was actually a form of exile from their true home, which they believed was the soul plane or the realm of their higher selves. It is no wonder that, trapped as they felt themselves in the smallness of their earthly lives, the soul plane was represented in tales and myths as a world of gods and giants.

As it is through woman, the womb of man, that we all find our way into physical existence, so we can name the path by which spirit was first able to condense itself down into matter, the female or yin path, and we can see that it was by this route that the 'spiritual seed' of humanity was first able to find its way, with many a backward glance, down on to the earthly plane. This time when our connection with the earth was the main goal of our evolutionary development is remembered in myth and legend as a time of a female-dominated, matriarchal society.

It has already been mentioned that the Earth can be likened to a beautiful woman with great power of attraction over her spiritual consort. Once spiritual evolution had reached the point where the female ray had been traversed and man was able to complete forming a downward connection between his soul and the mineral level of his being, this power of attraction became something of a problem. The time had come for mankind to start to work its way back up to the soul plane, creating as he did so a bridge between the material and the spiritual, so that all beings on whatever level their awareness resided would have access to a path which connected them and so could exist together in harmony knowing they were all linked in the vast being of the universe.

This crisis is described in the flood myths found in so many traditions and can be linked with stories of the lost continents of Atlantis and Mu. The problem was that mankind was likely to continue on his downward path as his soul was drawn more and more deeply into matter. The Earth provided the solution to this crisis by encasing a large portion of her 'attractive' or 'magnetic' power in the minerals that made up a small part of her body, and by tearing this from herself she was so able to stop the downward plunge of our souls before we became so deeply embedded on the material plane that we could never have risen from it again. This forms a basic pattern for many shamanic healing techniques still in use today, from cultures as diverse as the Australian Aborigines and South American Faith Healers.

The part of her self that Mother Earth sacrificed in this way is, of course, the Moon, the holder of the most ancient energies of the Earth, and interestingly enough thought by many scientists, because of this, to be older than the Earth, rather than, as is strictly correct, the oldest part of the Earth. By interposing her own body between the drawing power of the moon and the spiritual source of our solar system, our Father the sun, the Earth is able to regulate the rate at which we are pulled to her in a rhythmic way, so that we are able to work with a rhythmic flow of energy from spirit into matter and from matter back to spirit.

Phases of the Moon

It will be clear from this how important it is to be in touch with the phases of Grandmother Moon, as the Native Americans called her, and to understand how they affect us here on the Earth. It should be a simple matter to discover the phase of the moon from the daily newspaper, or a diary or calender, but, as in all shamanic work, information is no substitute for experience.

In order to work truly in harmony with the moon, you must spend as much time outside looking upon her face as you possibly can. Get to know where she will rise and set upon the horizon. Try to become familiar with her path through the night sky, but as you begin to feel the effect that she has upon us here on the Earth do not use her as an excuse for any problem times or bad days that you may have, but rather use your expanding awareness positively and creatively to bring your being into harmony with the natural tides of life.

Clearly, the full moon, when the sun is able to shine directly on the face of the moon, is the time when the pull of the physical world is at its strongest. It is a time when our physical 'doing' energy should be at its peak. It is a good time for actively getting on with things in a creative outward way.

Try to spend some time out of doors in the light of the full moon. Feel her magnetic pull working through every level of your being. Be aware of the unique way this affects you. Find your own link with the moon and ask her to share her energy with you. You could be amazed at the results.

As the Earth gradually interposes her body between the moon and sun, and the moon begins to wane, we may become aware of a change of emphasis as our ties to the physical world loosen and we begin to be drawn to the unmanifest side of things – matters of the soul and spirit. We should at this time be trying to work in harmony with the natural tides, and feed the energy and learning we have acquired through life in a physical body back to our souls in order that our higher selves may learn, grow and be strengthened, not depleted, by our present incarnations.

On the dark moon, when no light from the sun touches the moon and she is in fact no longer visible, we are loosened from the pull of the material world and have much easier access to the higher spiritual levels. This is traditionally a time of fasting and isolation, and is the origin of the separation of women from the rest of the tribe during their 'moon time' or menstruation, which would naturally fall at this point of the moon's cycle if one lived in perfect balance and harmony with the natural world.

You may find that meditation at this time is easier and more rewarding, and that your dreams are full of meaning. However, if you did not fully energise yourself on the full moon you may find that tiredness is a problem. Some traditions see the dark moon as a time of fear and 'black magic'. This is simply fear of the unseen side of things resulting from an alienation within ourselves from the unseen or spiritual side of our nature.

As the moon begins to wax again we are drawn gently back down to the Earth. Now is the time to try to draw down also all the wisdom and understanding that we have accumulated through repeated incarnations on the Earth, and that we have incorporated in our soul bodies. The illumination that the conscious guidance of our higher selves, or soul selves, can spread through our lives, can be likened to the difference between groping in the dark and walking in the sunlight.

MYTHS AND LEGENDS

Once man had fully traversed the female ray and was able to incarnate his soul in a body given to him by his Mother the Earth, the time had come to turn his attention heavenwards again so that by returning whence he came via the male ray the circle or circuit would be complete, and man would become a permanent bridge between heaven and earth. This theme can be traced through the myths and legends of so many cultures, from the longing to return to Eden in Jewish mythology, and the need for a 'messiah' to restore paradise in the Quetzalcoatl stories of the Aztecs or Pahana myths of Mesoamerica which bear an amazing resemblance to the ancient stories of the Chaldeans, Sumerians, Babylonians, Assyrians, Greeks, Egyptians and Romans.

At this time of change, after the birth of the moon, which was echoed in the loss of the great civilisations which are remembered in the legends of Atlantis and Mu, and which myth tells us were matriarchal in character, so they were based on the downward female ray and had to be destroyed in order that they didn't prevent man's necessary traversing of the male ray, many other great social changes took place. The matriarchal society, that has left its echo in the very ancient female deities of diverse cultures such as the Egyptian Isis, Cerridwen, Arianrod and Grania from Celtic myth, and Frigga and Hela from Norse mythology, and which archaeologists have found traces of in the many mother figurines that have been discovered all over the world, such as those found in Dolni Vestonice in Czechoslovakia, Brassempouy in France and Willendorf in Austria, was at an end, although much time passed before the Great Mother or the goddess was forgotten. Society gradually became patriarchal and the god or gods were worshipped in many cultures in recognition of the fact that the male or upward path back to our spiritual source was now of paramount importance to humankind.

In many of the remaining tribal societies surviving today such as that of the Iticoteri Indians in the jungle between Venezuela and Brazil, it is believed that women have no power of their own and must put themselves under the protection of the dominant male in the family. However a woman who does not marry, or an older woman who, after child bearing, takes back the responsibility for her own life, is often recognised as an extremely powerful shaman. An interesting example of this can be read about in Florinda Donner's book *Shabono*, in which she describes her experience of living with South American Indians.

What is actually happening is that women are deliberately putting aside their own power. Just as the Earth sacrificed a part of her body in order that the descent into matter could be slowed and a bridge built up so that matter could return to spirit, so woman deliberately stepped back in society so it could be guided by man who must lead in the task of taking matter back to spirit.

I think it is necessary at this stage to clarify three points. First, these changes in society did not take place overnight or as a result of conscious mental decisions. The understanding necessary for this direction to be chosen came from man's higher self, and so mankind was guided slowly and sometimes painfully along the path that it was necessary for him to take, rather as a parent guides a child through childhood, knowing that growing up is inevitable even if the child cannot yet see this, and that it must be helped along its path so that it too can become an adult. The only difference is that the parent we are talking about, in this case, is a part of ourselves.

The second point is that our souls, or higher selves, are androgynous, that is neither male nor female. Gender is mainly a characteristic of the physical body, although the sex of the physical body affects our emotional and mental bodies to some degree. Our higher selves incarnate in a body of whichever sex is appropriate to our life purpose and this is an indication of which ray, male or female, one has chosen primarily to work with during this one particular lifetime.

Third, it may appear from reading this chapter so far that I am under the illusion that humankind is the sole reason for all of creation. We all stand at the centre of our own circles and therefore the perspective that each of us has on the rest of the universe is that of looking out from the centre. It may appear that everything else fits around us, which in a way it does. It is necessary as a shaman, though, to be able to move your awareness and experience things from the perspective of others. Of course humankind is not of paramount importance in the scheme of the universe, but is a very necessary, integral part of things. As human beings we are attempting to understand ourselves and the part we are required to play in the scheme of things. We must not let this blind us to the importance of every other part of creation or to the interconnectedness of all things. We are already familiar with the fact that at the highest level all things, of whatever order, are one, and in our relationships with all things in the world around us we are actually relating to and experiencing an aspect of the infinite.

The Web of Life

In order to understand this point more fully it will help if we can experience for ourselves our own connections to the rest of the universe. In agreement with modern scientific thought, the shaman experiences all the world around as consisting of different levels of energy. We will now try to expand our awareness enough to become directly aware of the energy links that connect us to everything that is. Shamans in many traditions have used a spider's web as an analogy of these energy patterns and, despite our modern scientific understanding of energy connections, this remains the best way to experience this phenomenon.

Sit comfortably in your special place at a time when you can be undisturbed. Prepare yourself as explained in Chapter 1, and as you feel appropriate. Concentrate on your breathing until you feel totally calm and relaxed. Then, without opening your eyes, try to be aware of your immediate surroundings. I am describing the situation as though you are in a room in your home, but if you are at some outdoor power place then it will be a simple matter to adapt this. Choose first something that you know well, maybe a plant, a crystal or ornament. Try to feel your connection with this object.

Visualise or feel this connection as a fine fibre, which extends from your body to the object you are concentrating on. This may take a while, or even several attempts, before you feel sure enough to go any further. Do not rush, be content to go at your own pace. When you are certain of your awareness of this first connecting fibre, expand your awareness to encompass all the minerals, then the plants, then the objects around you which you have found meaning or power in. Build up, fibre by fibre, your awareness of the energy web which connects you to your immediate surroundings.

When you feel ready expand your awareness a little more, enough to encompass your entire house. Perhaps there are other people in the building. Feel your connection with each of them. Try to be aware of where the fibre leaves your body and where it joins theirs. Perhaps you have pets, so feel your connection with each of them, down to the smallest goldfish or stick insect. There are fibres which bind you to everything that lives within your home and, as the Native Americans teach, all that is has life. Become aware even of the fibres which bind you to the rocks in the ground upon which your house is built.

When you are ready expand your awareness a little further, to encompass the neighbourhood in which you live. Become aware of the fibres which connect you to each person, young and old, friend or foe. Feel your connection to each animal, whether in the air above or the ground beneath, to each plant from the tallest tree to the moss on the wall, and to the rocks and stones in the ground.

As your awareness expands to encompass the web of life you will find that you are rushing on without my guidance. Now you are aware of your connection to the whole of your country and now to all the Earth, but do not stop there. Expand your awareness now to encompass the entire solar system. Feel the fibres that bind you to your Mother the Earth and your Father the sun, but be aware also of those that bind you to the moon and each of the other planets, which are the physical manifestations of spiritual beings.

Now take one last leap of awareness and feel your connection to the entire universe. You are bound to every star and every planet, to all things seen and unseen, known and unknown. Feel the fibres. Know your place as an integral part of the web. Never again will you feel lost or alone, for you have experienced your place in the scheme of things. Wherever you are you are known and you are loved.

Now slowly let your awareness shrink back down again. Back to the solar system . . . back to the Earth . . . back to your country . . . back to your town . . . your house . . . your room and you in it. As your awareness shrinks back to its normal size know that your place on the web is not lost – things are still as you have just experienced them, you are simply no longer aware of them.

Do not rush out of this experience back to your everyday life, take time to have something to eat or drink and make sure you are firmly rooted once again in your everyday awareness of things before resuming your day-to-day tasks.

Having now experienced our place in the Universe, let us resume our examination of how we got here. The completion of the downward, female path and the birth of the moon marked mankind's firm connection with the Earth on his mineral level. As he worked his way up the male path through the plant level to the animal level, we see him change from a creature concerned mainly just with survival to one with a quite complex tribal social structure. This is, of course, linked with man's transition from a hunter-gatherer lifestyle to a settled agricultural being, who had the time and security to devote his life to more than just surviving. Much was lost with this transition, and man's closeness to the Earth and his oneness with the natural tides of life were necessary sacrifices in order that progress could be made.

The transition from the animal level to the mental level can be traced through recorded history. As humanity began to look on the world no longer as it was, but as it might become, as they began to think about their individual rights before the good of the community as a whole, we see a gradual change taking place. Although the Industrial Revolution could give us a clear date for this transition, its beginnings can be traced for many hundred years before this and its completion was by no means overnight.

Humankind now stands firmly rooted on the fourth or mind level, having to a large extent forgotten where they have come from or, for that matter, where they are supposed to be going. The desperate search for spiritual identity of so many people today, the urge to escape into space and the destructive capabilities of modern technology are all symptoms of people trapped on the fourth level. But all is not lost, for those who know where to look the beginnings of our transition to the fifth level are already evident. Political initiatives towards peace and the breaking down of national barriers are a good sign. The New Age of spiritual and ethical values outweighing personal gain is beginning to dawn. This is what humankind as a whole must work towards. Let us hope that the fifth level of soul awareness can be achieved in time to avert the crisis to the brink of which our limited fourth level perspective has led us.

I have been told that the whole of humankind's development, as just described, has actually been a brief recap of what took place in other worlds at different stages of our learning and evolution, in fact during previous cycles of creation. I put this forward as nothing more than an interesting idea. For me this is fourth level information, unlike the rest of this book which is an understanding of what I have accumulated over many lifetimes which I am able to bring down from my soul level through my mind level, and so pass on to others in the form of a book. I feel it is almost certain that the Earth exists as a result of the successful completion of the female ray by many spiritual beings who then divided to follow their own particular paths of evolution, humankind being just one of these. So it is more than likely that the first part of our time upon the Earth was in fact a replay of something that had happened over a much vaster timescale, rather as the developing body of a foetus in its mother's womb relives the entire physical evolution of its species, whether it be a rat or a human.

These ideas, however interesting, have little relevance to us today. The timescale of humankind's evolution is totally irrelevant. It is the direction and the sequence which we need to understand in order to shamanically balance and harmonise our lives today, and be ready to stride confidently into tomorrow.

Let us examine now, then, a way in which our new understanding can be linked in a practical way with our contemporary lives. It has already been mentioned how the body of a developing child in the first few weeks in its mother's womb relives the entire physical evolution of the human body, from a single celled plant-like creature, through a fish-like phase, through amphibian and repitilian-like development until it resembles a small mammal, and gradually its tail is absorbed into its body and it becomes a miniature human being. Similarly, during our childhood and adolescence, we re-enact the entire spiritual evolution of humankind.

When our higher self decides it is time again to experience life on the material plane it connects with the Earth, through the already complete female ray and, with the help of the being it has chosen to be its mother, it builds up its own mineral connection with the Earth. By the time this is complete the soul has, with help, condensed itself sufficiently to have firmly linked itself with the miniature body with which its parents have provided it. This is the time of birth. The child enters the world through the gateway between the physical and the mineral levels – its mother's base chakra. It is now ready to start traversing the male ray and growing up.

The level through which the developing child has next to grow is the physical, and for the first seven years of its life it will be building the basis for its plant self. This does not mean that a child under the age of seven has no feelings, or any of the qualities associated with the heart or animal level, nor does it mean that it has no mind or any of the qualities associated with the human level. These levels are there waiting to be reached at the right time. They can only be accessed at this stage through the physical, and should certainly not, as in many contemporary child-rearing practices, be directly approached, as this will detract the flow of vital etheric or life energy from the child's body and will lead to life-long weakness on this level. Paediatric studies of young children show that they become emotionally attached or bonded with whoever usually feeds, clothes and physically comforts them. Likewise they learn by imitating the world around them – by doing, rather than by intellectual explanations. We can therefore see that both the mental and emotional levels of the developing child during the first seven years of its life are dependent upon, and must be reached through, its physical energy body.

By the child's seventh year, and again this is no rigidly fixed date, the child has, if allowed to develop in a natural way, completed building its physical or etheric energy body, and is ready to commence working on its animal or heart level, and building up its emotional energy body. As with the physical body the incarnating soul already has a basic framework within which to build.

It has been noted by many child psychiatrists, educationalists and paediatricians, such as Piagett and Steiner, for example, that around the age of seven a child begins to relate to the world in a very different way. The child realises that what it does not see or directly experience can still exist. The child understands its place within its immediate family and social surroundings, no longer experiencing itself as the centre of all things, but now being able to reach out and communicate with those around it in a feeling, caring way. The child now begins to feel emotional attachments to people and things it admires, but which have no direct influence upon the child's well-being. This is the time of heros, best friends, dragons to be slain, wrongs to be righted and quests to be undertaken. All children, as they build up their emotional bodies, live in the days of fairy tales and sagas. Given a chance they will love and emulate the good and beautiful, and fear and hate what they experience as bad. If not given a chance, if surrounded by our technological world where they are unable to differentiate between reality and fraud, truth and deceit, right and wrong, if they have imposed upon them our adult shades of grey, our fourth level explanations and understandings, they will still do their best to build up an emotional body that will allow them to function in the world as they experience it. This may, however, be a rather distorted thing which exhibits the limits and checks that the world has imposed upon their growth, rather than being a true expression of who and what they really are.

Again this is not to say that children from the age of about seven to fourteen, or puberty, are not capable of using their minds. On the contrary they can learn a great deal during this period of their lives, but anyone who has been involved in teaching children, either in a formal situation or simply as a caring adult, will have realised that if you can make the child care about the subject which you are trying to teach, that is get them emotionally involved in what they are doing, then your only problem is keeping up with them. However, if you attempt to teach in the dry, intellectual way that would be appropriate for older children you may well have a revolution on your hands! Their minds must be approached through their emotional energy bodies, since to approach them directly results in diverting the child's energies from their emotional energy body and causing weakness on that level – in my experience a very common problem.

By the time the incarnating soul has been on the Earth about fourteen years it should have completed building its emotional energy body, although as with the physical energy body the child will still have some growing to do on this level. The child's entry into the fourth or adult world is heralded by many changes, and it can be seen as rather a shock to their entire system! With puberty a young person gains a totally new outlook on the world. What before was accepted and lived with it is now possible to question, challenge and possibly change. The child again becomes the centre of his or her own world – there are close links between the fourth and the second world in this respect. This is the time for formal intellectual learning. If the child has developed in a balanced way up to this point the world now becomes their oyster. There is nothing the child cannot do, and nothing is too sacred to be held up to the cold, hard light of day, and examined and questioned. Let us hope that much of what has so far been given to build the child's life with will be found to be good and true. Some souls at this stage firmly shut the door to the lower levels of themselves, unable to cope with what they find there. Yet others retreat back to those lower worlds, unable to cope with the challenge of the fourth world.

From the age of fourteen to twenty-one the young person builds his or her mental energy body. The young person lives totally through the fourth or human level (that is assuming that childhood so far has been such that he or she has been able to progress to this point in a reasonably balanced healthy state), in the fourth world of humankind's evolutionary development. The young person has caught up with the rest of humankind! The question is what will he or she do next?

As we have already seen now is the time for the advent of the fifth world. The fourth world is balancing on the brink of every kind of disaster our narrow human viewpoint can bring it to. Will we be able to take the step upward that is required of us so that we have conscious access to our soul levels and can live our lives from the viewpoint of our higher selves? In doing so we would be taking the first step into the fifth world, a gateway that we should all reach during our twenty-first year on the Earth. As tradition tells us, at twenty-one we have the key of the door. We seem to have forgotten what door this is. How many of us will have the courage to unlock the door of our crown chakras and step through into the fifth world?

In the fourth world we experience ourselves, our egos, as being centred in our minds. We go through our lives as minds with bodies and emotions attached to them. On attaining fifth level awareness we begin to realise that the true seat of the ego or self is in fact the soul. We begin to experience ourselves as souls with minds, hearts and bodies to inhabit and care for. This level of awareness has been described in many religions, but whatever terminology we have been taught to use to describe it – enlightenment, Christ awareness, Buddha awareness etc. – whatever path we have trodden to reach it, the experience is fundamentally the same. As the myths of different cultures have used different imagery to describe the same truths, so different teachers through the ages have described the different paths they have taken towards fifth level awareness. The mistake of their followers has been to assume that the path that they have been taught to follow is the only one.

We live at a unique point in history. Never before has there been a time when it has been possible for us to choose our own path. In the past we were born into a particular culture or religion which we either followed or rejected at our peril. Even if we could change our religion, it was usually only to follow another religious code of practice or the path laid down by a particular

teacher. Today we are spoilt for choice. For the spiritual con-
sumer there are so many paths to salvation on the market that
we must assume that the only reason that we are not yet all in
the fifth world must be either lack of interest or lack of the
correct currency!

If you have read thus far then I am sure you will have realised
that the only path that will get you to fifth level awareness is
your own unique path. I am attempting in this book to shed
some light upon that path, but only you can really tell what
works for you. By all means look around and see what's on offer,
but do not lose awareness of who you are, where you've been
and where you're going. If you see or hear of something that
you feel may help you in your endeavours, then by all means try
it. But try it on your terms. Beware of anything that claims to
be exclusive of all else or anyone who claims to know what is
best for you. You have a guide or teacher within you, your own
higher self, who has been with you since the beginning of time.
He or she has guided you down the female ray into physical
existence and now, with your teacher's guidance, you have nearly
succeeded in journeying back up the male ray to the point at
which you can again be united with your true self. Use all you
can to assist yourself towards this end, but do not allow anything
to stop you now. You are so close!

In the next chapter we will examine the shamanic technique
for experiencing directly the different levels of ourselves which
will help us strengthen the bridge that we are trying to create.
We will also learn to draw closer to our higher selves and take
direct guidance from them. But let us take a few moments first
to consider the practical applications of what we have learnt in
this chapter.

To realise that you have not been alone in your growth and
development can in itself be a healing discovery. By understanding the overall purpose of the different phases of childhood we
can begin to realise where our weaknesses may lie, and begin
the process of healing and rebalancing them. Hopefully we will
also become more understanding and compassionate towards
others, knowing the common path we have all trodden. For those

directly involved in child care the implications are enormous. To work consciously in direct cooperation with the higher self of an incarnating child in order to give the soul which has entrusted itself into your care the best chance possible of achieving its life purpose should be the aim of all parents and teachers. Then perhaps our generation will be the last that needs to read books about self-healing and realisation!

The information given in this chapter could either be a new and fascinating theory of evolution or a rather far-fetched fantasy. Either way, what relevance does it have to your life? The purpose of this book is not to fill people's heads with interesting ideas: it is rather to change lives. The reason for imparting the above information is to expand your awareness of yourself and the world around you in order that you may have a deeper and more meaningful perspective on your own life and interaction with those around you.

If you cannot accept the contents of this chapter question where that reaction is coming from. Perhaps in order to 'learn' the above you will have to 'unlearn' a great deal of your past programming. Try looking around you at friends, relatives and acquaintances. Although humankind, as a whole, is now at the threshold of the fifth world, that is not to say that each individual has reached a uniform point in their own personal development. Although the awareness of each human being resides primarily in their own mental body, just as the awareness of animals is mainly (but not totally) in their emotional or instinctive body, and plants in their physical body, that is not to say that each person's mental body is as strong or as highly evolved as their other energy bodies.

Someone who is concerned only with their own physical welfare and pleasures, who makes sensation the main aim of their life and seems to care for no one but him or herself is mainly living through the second or plant level of their own personal evolution. This does not mean that they are 'evil' or inferior in any way. It simply means that in this lifetime that person is working mainly with that level of him or herself for reasons that no one but their own higher self can know.

A person who lives mainly through their feelings and instincts, who is totally involved in their own family or clan, and cannot extend their awareness beyond what immediately touches themselves and the circle of people around them, is living mainly in the third world of their own personal development. Just as the second world is the level of self-awareness, this third world is the level of tribal awareness. The fourth world is the level of national, or political, awareness and it can be seen that the dawning fifth world will be the level of global awareness.

So, how will your new understanding affect the way you react to the people around you? First, and most importantly, it must not be used as a way of judging people or in any way categorising them. Nobody can know the karmic purpose of anybody else's life. The 'human vegetable', unable to move or in any way interact with the world around, with no apparent awareness of their own being, may well be a highly evolved soul who simply needed one more lifetime in which to strengthen the mineral level of their own being before being reborn on to the Earth as a great healer or teacher.

This understanding of evolution shows that there is reason and purpose in all our lives, and therefore should teach us to approach every other being with respect and understanding rather than judgement or condemnation. Not only will you learn to recognise the different levels of yourself and how they work together, but you will eventually be able to understand the delicate balance in the people and relationships around you.

You will also be able to choose on which level to relate to other people, rather than, as usually happens, simply to interact on the lowest common level! You will begin to know when people around you are trapped within a particular level of themselves and by reaching out to them on another level you may be able to help free them. You may well be the kind of person who does all this anyway, without really knowing how or why. Well, now is the time to become consciously aware of what you are doing.

And if all of this still seems too far-fetched to contemplate then go on to the next chapter and when you have learnt to establish a conscious link with your own higher self ask him or her to give you a picture of evolution that you can accept and work with. In other words, find your own truth!

Chapter 3
NON-ORDINARY REALITY

The woman and her daughters lighted candles and placed them in the window recesses and at the head of the corpse. Then they went into their dormer-room and left Sheen to her watching. She sat at the fire and made one faggot after another blaze up. She had brought her basket of bog-down and she began to spin a thread upon the neighbour woman's wheel.

She finished the thread and put it around her neck. Then she began to search for more candles so that she might be able to light one, as another went out. But as she rose up all the candles went out at once. The hound started from the foot of the bed. Then she saw the corpse sitting up stiffly in the place where it had been laid.

Something in Sheen overcame her dread, and she went over to the corpse and took the salt that was on its breast and put it on its lips. Then a voice came from between the lips 'Fair maid,' said the voice, 'have you the courage to follow me? The others failed me and they have been stricken. Are you faithful?' 'I will follow you,' said Sheen. 'Then,' said the corpse, 'put your hands on my shoulders and come with me. I must go over the Quaking Bog, and through the Burning Forest, and across the Icy Sea.' Sheen put her hands on his shoulders. A storm came and they were swept through the roof of the house. They were carried through the night. Down they came on the ground and the dead man sprang away from Sheen. She went to follow him and found her feet upon a shaking sod. They were on the Quaking Bog, she knew. The corpse of the Hunter-King went ahead and she knew that she must keep it in sight. He went swiftly. The sod went under her feet and she was in the watery mud. She struggled out and jumped over a pool that was hidden with heather. All the time she was in dread that the figure that went before her so quickly would be lost to her. She sank and she struggled and she sprang across pools and morasses. All the time what had been the corpse of the Hunter-King went before her.

Then she saw fires against the sky and she knew they were coming to the Burning Forest. The figure before her sprang across a ditch and went into the forest. Sheen sprang across it too. Burning branches fell across her path as she went on. Hot winds burnt her face. Flames dazzled and smoke dazed her. But the figure before her went straight on too.

The forest ended on a cliff. Below was the sea. The figure before her dived down, and Sheen dived too. The cold chilled her to the marrow. She thought the chill would drive the life out of her. But she saw the head of one swimming before her and she swam on.

And then they were on land again. 'Fair Maid,' said the corpse of the Hunter-King, 'put your hands on my shoulders again.' She put her hands on his shoulders. A storm came and swept them away. They were driven through the roof of the neighbour woman's house. The candle wicks fluttered and light came on them again. She saw the hound standing in the middle of the floor. She saw the corpse sitting where it had been laid and the eyes were now open.

'Fair maid,' said the voice of the Hunter-King, 'you have brought me back to life. I am a man under enchantment. There is a witch-woman in the wood that I gave my love to. She enchanted me so that the soul was out of my body, and wandering away. It was my soul you followed. And the enchantment was to be broken when I found a heart so faithful that it would follow my soul over the Quaking Bog, through the Burning Forest, and across the Icy Sea. You have brought my soul and my life back to me.' Then she ran out of the neighbour's house.

Extract from **The King of Ireland's Son**, *Padraic Colum (Floris Books), a retelling of an Irish Celtic story, and also a classic example of shamanic journeying*

In the last two chapters we explored the nature of human beings and their purpose on the earth, and, in particular, who you are and why you are here. It has been stated several times that shamans learn by direct experience. You have, hopefully, already worked through exercises and tasks designed to expand your awareness. Now it is time to take the next step, and learn to direct and control your awareness using the technique commonly called shamanic journeying. It must be stressed that we will be learning a technique that will enable us to become aware (usually, but by no means always, through the medium of dream-like imagery), of what already exists. We will not be trying deliberately to create these images, but simply experience them. This is quite different from visualisation techniques where images are imagined or created.

Shamanic journeying is a deliberate, structured and controlled exploration of non-ordinary reality. In order to understand what non-ordinary reality is we must first examine what the reality that we experience as ordinary really is. The usual answer to this would be that anything which is perceived with the five senses of sight, hearing, taste, smell and touch can be considered as ordinary reality. It will immediately be obvious to most people, though, that there are such varying degrees of sensitivity by which different people experience these senses, that what may be ordinary for one person may well be quite extraordinary for another! For instance, to a person who has been blind all their life colour would be in the realms of non-ordinary reality. Similarly, to people who have lived their lives in a tribal situation, close to the Earth and aware of the spiritual realities of life, ordinary reality would consist of much that would seem to modern-day people non-ordinary. The Native Americans and the Australian Aborigines were both astounded and horrified that the invaders of their lands could simply not perceive what made their holy places and sacred sites special.

In the past it was far more commonly understood that to some people reality was a much vaster thing than others were able to perceive. It is only relatively recently that reality has been standardised and defined. *The Oxford English Dictionary* definition of reality is as follows: 'Property of being real, resemblance to the original; real existence, what is real, what underlies appearances.' This seems to hint that our modern view of only what we can directly perceive as being valid is totally wrong. What we consider real only 'resembles the original'. What is the original? Reality is actually 'what underlies appearance', and this is how we can define what has come to be known as non-ordinary reality. In ordinary reality we are physical beings which resemble our original, or true, selves. In non-ordinary reality we are beings of many different levels, as we have already seen. Likewise, the world around us which it is considered normal or ordinary for one to perceive is simply a world of appearances and in order to experience directly the reality behind this appearance we must learn to work in the realms of (non-ordinary) reality.

Much misunderstanding of the religious and spiritual lives of what we consider to be primitive peoples has taken place as a result of these two different understandings of reality. To our ancient ancestors, and to many recently studied 'primitive' people, reality meant the higher truths hidden behind physical appearances. To the modern-day historians and anthropologists who studied them this was incomprehensible, since to them reality was what could be directly perceived by means of their five senses, most of which incidentally are head-based and firmly fixed within our fourth level understanding of things, and anything beyond this was childish imagination. Even our modern-day science is rooted in this appearance level understanding of reality. If it cannot be seen, touched, quantified or measured, then it is at best considered as a theory – the scientific term for imagination – while at worst it is totally dismissed, as has been the case with so much of our spiritual heritage.

It will be clear that the tasks given in Chapter 1 and the meditational exercise given in Chapter 2 have all been helping you to explore non-ordinary reality. If you are happy with your progress so far, then now is the time to try to experience it in a more direct way. If you have not been as successful as you may have hoped so far, then perhaps a more direct approach would suit you. Do not rush. Read through this chapter several times before attempting anything and be sure you understand exactly what you are doing. There is no danger at all involved in the method of shamanic journeying I will describe. As we have already seen we exist in ordinary reality – the world of appearances – and non-ordinary reality – we are in fact far more than we appear to be. So, by moving our awareness into non-ordinary reality we are simply experiencing directly a part of ourselves which is already there but of which we are not normally aware.

In ancient times, although most people were far more aware of non-ordinary reality than is common today, it was left to the shamans to learn to operate in this dimension. In some societies these abilities were left to develop more or less naturally, and a shaman would pick a successor from the most promising up-and-coming shaman in the village, passing on a few secret techniques, perhaps, but not attempting to contain or manipulate the student's natural gift. In other societies, however, shamanic learning was found to be a saleable commodity and methods were found to help even the most unlikely student to experience reality in a non-ordinary way. In some cases, after drug-induced expansion of perception the student then learned how to control his or her own awareness and went on to become a powerful shaman. Far more commonly the student who needed to resort to this artificial method of expanding their awareness became hopelessly dependent upon the plant or plants used for this purpose with a subsequent loss of personal power and integrity.

Whatever the training methods used, techniques of shamanic journeying, that is the ability to operate deliberately and consciously in non-ordinary reality, are remarkably similar all around the world. To gain access to the Lower World, that is the level below the fourth, mind level at which our awareness usually resides, Eskimo shamans, operating in non-ordinary reality, went down through a hole in the ice, while Australian Aborigines found access through a cave and the Northern European shamans travelled down through the roots of a tree. To embark upon a comparative study of worldwide shamanic techniques is beyond the scope of this book, but for the student who wishes to pursue this line of enquiry I recommend Roger N Walsh's book *The Spirit of Shamanism*, which is a very accessible, yet in-depth study of comparative shamanism.

As stated before the best method of shamanic study is practical. No amount of information is a substitute for direct experience. With the intention of experiencing shamanic journeying for ourselves, then, let us now examine the tools the shaman traditionally used for this purpose, and their relevance and practical applications for the modern-day shamanic worker.

Shamanic Tools

As described in Chapter 1, before starting any form of shamanic work it is advisable to cleanse oneself and the environment one is working in of any negativity which may have accumulated during the course of everyday life. This is traditionally done by burning a herbal smudge mix, the smoke of which is purifying. Native Americans used prairie sage for this purpose, while Northern European traditions favoured the herb rosemary. Christian and Eastern traditions used frankincense. None of these will work without the directed intention of the shaman. So the first and foremost tool of the shaman is him or herself. No tool you can use will have any more power than that which you are able to invest in it. Your safeguard and the channel through which this power is able to flow is your will or your intention. Never attempt shamanic work when you are angry, resentful or unsure of your true intentions. Spend your time and energy harmonising and rebalancing yourself. Don't rush. Only you can know when your intention is genuine and pure. As stated before, this is your first and most powerful tool, and the only one which is totally indispensable. Be absolutely sure of it before you proceed any further.

Choose whichever smudge mix you prefer. Either buy it ready-made, or preferably try mixing your own, which will probably work more powerfully and harmoniously with you. Ordinary garden sage, such as can be bought from most supermarkets, has similar properties to its North American counterpart. Dried rosemary is similarly available. Frankincense is a little harder to obtain and is expensive. Dried lavender, cedar and sweetgrass are all thought to aid in attracting positive energies. A small amount of dried herbs can be set alight and smouldered in a suitable container or, if this proves difficult, charcoal blocks, indented for burning incense, can be used. Feel free to experiment with different mixes until you find the one that works best for you.

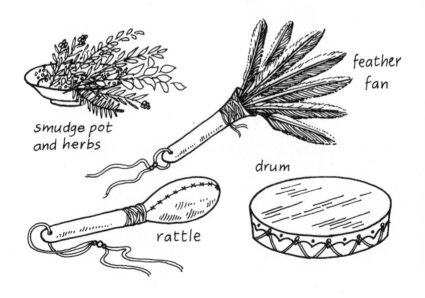

feather fan

smudge pot and herbs

drum

rattle

Most shamans use a fan or feather of some sort to direct the smudge smoke. Again this is a fairly easy tool to craft for yourself. A country walk in late summer should provide you with a good selection of feathers to bind together to form a beautiful and functional tool. It goes without saying that animal products which have been obtained by any method which involves exploitation and suffering to the animals involved should not be used.

The two tools which are most commonly associated with shamanic journeying are the rattle and the drum. Many modern day shamans, however, dispense with these to some extent by using a pre-recorded drumming tape which is certainly more socially acceptable to their neighbours! Both the drum, and especially the rattle, have far more uses than those described here. We shall now examine their uses only as applies to shamanic journeying techniques.

The drum is sometimes described as the shaman's horse. It is the beat, or the vibration, of the drum that the shaman's awareness uses consciously to propel itself from one form of reality to another. This can perhaps be better understood by referring back to the different energy bodies that we all possess as described above. All energy moves. It has its own particular vibration or rhythm. The rhythm of your heart beat, closely linked to that of your breath, is the rhythm or vibrational pattern of your physical body. Your emotional body has a slightly faster rhythm and your mental body vibrates even faster. To be aware of all levels of being, in both ordinary and non-ordinary reality, however, is a function of the soul. Therefore the level of ourselves to which we must attune ourselves in order to be able to commence shamanic journeying is the soul level and one of the best methods for doing this is by using a drum beat of the correct vibrational frequency.

It will now be obvious, as we stand on the threshold of the fifth world, why shamanic journeying, a function of our fifth, soul levels, comes so easily to us today. For our ancestors, at a different point in mankind's evolutionary development it was quite a different matter. The ancient shaman may have had to prepare for months or even years before being able to attune sufficiently with the pattern of his or her soul to be able effectively to operate in non-ordinary reality.

This would also be a suitable point at which to mention the different effects that music can have. It would be too complex at this stage to consider pitch and harmony, but simply with this new understanding of rhythm it will be clear why so many young people feel 'spaced out' after listening to loud music with a fast beat, and also why they seem almost to become addicted to it. Music can be a very powerful tool in aligning and harmonising the different levels of our being. For instance, slow music can be very centring, earthing and relaxing. But used irresponsibly, without any clear understanding of what one is doing, it can be disruptive and harmful. Beware of the people who know just what they are doing, and would use their knowledge to manipulate and control you.

Either buy or make a rattle; something fairly light and easy to hold such as a dried gourd is ideal. Try using it to sense the different vibrational patterns of your energy bodies. Hold the rattle loosely in whichever hand it feels most comfortable. Allow it to move almost of its own accord. It is merely extending and amplifying your own sensitivity, it has no power beyond that which you invest in it. Be clear in your intention to tune in to, in turn, each of your different energy bodies. Besides pulsating, you will find that different energies also move in a spiral wave pattern. You will find, as you become experienced in the use of the rattle, that almost automatically, according to your intention, the rattle picks out these different wave patterns and moves with them.

Try rattling over your friends. Apart from being good practice for you it will be a most pleasant experience for them. As you become more experienced you may discover areas of disharmony in either your own or your friends' energy bodies. With the clear intention of reharmonising, rattle again, until all trace of the disharmony has gone. You may not ever know quite what it was that you were rebalancing, but I assure you that the effect will be felt in one way or another.

Shamanic Journeying

Shamanic journeying is the name given to the method by which a shaman experiences and moves in non-ordinary reality. I give here two different methods of shamanic journeying. The first makes use of a pre-recorded drumming tape. You could either make your own by drumming in the way described in method two or purchase one of the several versions on the market. (An address is given at the end of the book for purchasing mail-order drumming tapes.) Unless you have a friend to help you with the drumming method one is probably the best for a beginner as you can be completely relaxed without any distractions.

 METHOD ONE

Work in a place where you can be warm and comfortable, at a time when you can be sure not to be disturbed. You will need enough space to lie down.

Smudge both yourself and the area in which you are to work, then sit down comfortably and breathe rhythmically until you feel completely relaxed, and in harmony with yourself and your surroundings.

If you feel sufficiently competent in the use of the rattle now would be a good time to rattle around yourself with the *intention* of *harmonising*.

When you feel ready lie down and cover your eyes with a scarf or eye shield so no light reaches them. Make sure you know, however, where the switch is that will start your drumming tape. If you are worried about disturbing your family or neighbours it would be a good idea to wear headphones. Put these on now. If you are at all cold cover yourself with a blanket, so that your body will be completely comfortable and so relax, releasing your awareness from it.

Visualise yourself in a safe place somewhere in the natural world where you feel happy and secure. It can be either a place you know well, a place dimly remembered or somewhere entirely imaginary. In this place there will need to be either a pool of water, a well, a cave opening, a rabbit hole or a hollow tree – in effect some opening that will lead you downwards. If there is not something of this nature in the place you have chosen, then create one. When the drumming starts you are going to enter the Earth by the gateway you have visualised with the *intention* of *shamanically journeying to the Lower World and observing it.*

The Lower World is the term traditionally used by shamans from many different parts of the world to describe what the Native Americans called the third world, that which is directly below the fourth world of mind awareness in which we normally live. You will, in actual fact, be moving in non-ordinary reality to your third level, that of your inner child or your animal self. For the moment we are concerned mainly with your ability to do this, rather than what you will do once you are there. So, once having arrived have a look around and then return.

It must be stated again at this point that shamanic journeying is quite different from visualisation techniques with which you may be familiar. Visualisation is a function of the fourth, mind, level of ourselves, whereas shamanic journeying, as we have already seen, is a function of the fifth level. When shamanic journeying, once entering the tunnel or whatever you choose to use to symbolise the energy vortex between one level of being and the next you *experience* what happens rather than visualising or imagining. Therefore, you may simply have a feeling of travelling downwards rather than actually seeing. You may just know what is happening rather than seeing it all played out before you as on a TV screen. Your five senses do not operate here, for you have gone beyond them, but in order to make sense of what you have experienced, to start with at least, you will have to interpret it in terms of the senses you are familiar with. Thus, although you may say afterwards that you 'saw' something this cannot be true because your eyes were closed! Actually you experienced something and the only way you are able to describe this experience in terms of the fourth world is as if you saw it.

If you completely understand what you are going to do, and feel happy and confident about it, then switch on your drumming tape now.

If you feel worried, unsure or confused then read through this section again and take time to think about it. I give no techniques in this book that will take you out of your own energy system. All that you are doing is experiencing yourself in a new way. Anything that you encounter in this journey already exists within you. If you do not like what you find, or feel it is in any way hostile or threatening to you, then simply tell it to go away. You are in charge here, do not creep about like a thief in the dark, you are the master or mistress in your own house. You have a right to be here, as well as a very important need to expand and experience yourself in this way.

If you still feel unsure, but would nevertheless like to attempt shamanic journeying you could either work with a friend who has already learnt to journey effectively or you could work with an experienced teacher (details of workshops are given at the end of the book). I should also issue a word of caution here, though, which is that much of what is currently being taught as shamanic journeying is merely a form of visualisation and, although I do not criticize visualisation as such, it takes place purely in your fourth, mind level and will not get you anywhere outside of that, as visualisation is a function of the mind. If anyone tries to tell you what you see or experience either in your tunnel or in the lower world, then either they are invading your personal space, which no person of integrity would attempt to do without your permission or, as is more likely, they simply do not know what shamanic journeying really is.

When you are ready to return, either respond to the return signal on your tape or, if you are ready before that, return the way you came, back up through your tunnel to your special place. Most people find the return journey is much quicker and easier than the outward one. Take your time to gradually deepen your breathing and reaccustom your eyes to the light before sitting up.

Write up notes of your experience immediately, before you forget anything. If you find this difficult, or if your journeys become so rich in detail that you have difficulty in remembering everything then you could try speaking out your experiences as they happen and either asking a friend to note them down, or else recording them.

Do not worry if you are not successful on your first attempt. You are developing a new skill and many people find it takes repeated attempts to get them through the tunnel and into the lower world. Often this is simply a case of learning to trust and accept what you experience as genuine. Self-doubt is often an initial problem – it was certainly one of mine! Persevere, and soon your experiences will become too strong to be denied.

 METHOD TWO

This is the method of journeying I prefer to use whenever possible. It is not the method I initially learnt and I do not recommend it as the easiest method for beginners, unless for any reason they do not wish to try method one or, having tried it, they have been unsuccessful and feel that this method may suit them better.

You will need a rattle and a drum. I suggest that you take time to become familiar with these two tools so that you feel comfortable and confident in using them. You will also need a friend to drum for you, unless you are experienced enough to be able to journey while drumming yourself.

Prepare yourself by smudging and relaxing as in method one. When you are ready pick up your rattle and stand up. You are going to use the rattle to attune to the vibrational rate of your soul body. With this intention clearly in your mind let the rattle begin to move of its own accord. Move about, or dance, as you feel appropriate. Let the rattle move up, down or around as it wants. There is no rush, take as long over this as you need. You will know when you find the right rhythm. As a check, although everybody is unique, it will be somewhere about 200 to 220 beats per minute. When you find this rhythm your drummer can start playing along. When you feel ready, lie down, cover your eyes and commence your journey as described in method one. Your *intention* will be to shamanically journey to the Lower World to observe.

If you have no drummer, when you are sure of your rhythm put down your rattle, sit comfortably, take up your drum and commence drumming to the same rhythm. You should either sit in a darkened room, or wear a scarf or eye shield over your eyes. Be as relaxed and comfortable as possible, but do not falter in your drumming. Fix your intention firmly in your mind and commence journeying as described above.

Continue as described in method one.

Further Journeys

 **LOWER WORLD**

Having successfully reached the Lower World and observed what is there, the *intention* for a suitable second journey would be to 'visit the Lower World and bring back an object that has meaning to me'. Journey by whichever method works best for you. You will know what to bring back when you see it. You may find it is given to you or you may have to search for it. Whatever it is, when you find it hold it to you and return the way you came. On your return to ordinary reality you will find, of course, that you no longer have the object with you. Or do you? You may not have the physical appearance of the object, but you will have the 'original' form of that object which could be defined as an energy form. I suggest you find a physical form in which to lodge it, even if all you can manage is a rough sketch of the object. In all likelihood you will not have to search too far. Many people have found that by the 'strangest coincidence' over the course of the next few days after doing this journey the object that they brought back with them finds its way to them in its physical form. Some people, though, find they have to expend some effort in the search and this can be a lesson in itself.

Once you have your object, what can you learn from it? The first object that I brought back from a shamanic journey was a birds' nest. Two days later the physical form of my nest arrived in circumstances so similar to those by which I obtained it during my journey that I could not mistake it. Over the next few days I pondered over what a nest symbolised to me and what I should learn from it. I came to see it as a place of nurturing and protection; a safe place in which to grow; a place to fly out from when the time is right. When, at about that time, a space became available for me to devote purely to my shamanic work I realised that this was to be my nest – a place of refuge from the demands of my day-to-day life where I was to hatch out my power and grow to maturity in a way that I could not at that time even begin to imagine!

One of my students once brought back a stone flower from this, her second, shamanic journey. She was a little upset as she felt that this was in some way wrong, since the flower should have been a living, growing thing, not turned to stone. She neverthe-less made a flower from clay in which to lodge the energy form of her flower. Over the next few months, in her journeying and in her everyday life I watched her struggle to bring back to life a part of her which had always been denied and had effectively been turned to stone. It is strange that, at the time when it became obvious to both of us that she had succeeded in her struggle and she was able to connect to the vast power potential that she had at this level of herself by finding her own power animal, that her young son found her stone flower, and acci-dently shattered it.

 ## POWER ANIMALS

I suggest that the *intention* for your third shamanic jour-ney should be to journey to the Lower World to obtain a power animal.

As discussed in Chapter 1 the third level of yourself is your animal level, and just as you have already found the mineral and the plant that resonate the most strongly with your own mineral and plant levels, in order to know yourself more thoroughly and be able to work more effectively, you are now going to search for the form which expresses most closely your animal self. This is traditionally referred to as your power animal, as it is from this third level that your personal strengths or power come. Your own particular power animal can teach you much about your own unique power and how it can be most effectively used. Deliberately seeking your own power and bringing it forth into your everyday life can completely transform the way you live. You will ini-tially be looking for only one animal, but it is quite pos-sible to have more than one power animal. You may work for a certain amount of time with one power animal which will then be replaced as you progress sufficiently to work with a potential power that you had hitherto been unable to bring through into your life. Often more power animals will be discovered as you develop your shamanic abilities, but your principal one will always remain the closest to you.

Be quite clear that your power animal already exists, in potential at least, within you. You are not searching outside of yourself, nor are you calling to yourself the 'spirits' of any animals, either alive or dead! On discovering your power animal you may well find that you have a deep affinity for that species of animal. You will need to study it very closely in order to learn about yourself and how to use your power effectively. For instance, if your power takes the form of an eagle, rather than meeting any problems you may have in your life head on, you would be better advised to use your ability of flight to rise above them, and your clear-sightedness to fully understand them and so use them as landmarks in your life. Alternatively, if your power animal is a deer use your nimbleness and speed to good effect, ignore those who counsel more thought and a methodical approach to things, as that is simply not your way.

It may be that your power takes the form of an animal from myth or legend. If this is so then you must search for knowledge and understanding of your power from story books rather than natural history books. I do urge you to learn all you can of your power animal and what it means to you before turning to one of the books (several of which are listed in the bibliography at the end of this book) which attempt to interpret it for you. We are, after all, talking about *your* power animal and, just as you are a unique being, so your power, the way you understand it and the way you utilise it are unique.

One of my own power animals, which came to me at a time of transition in my life, is a unicorn. Traditionally the unicorn will only willingly come to a virgin. As a mother of four children I wondered if mine had made a slight mistake! Tracing the roots of the word, however, I discovered that a virgin was originally understood to be a woman who owns herself, rather than being the property of any man, regardless of whom she sleeps with. Its coming to me at that time as I was trying to free myself from a stereotyped woman's lifestyle felt like a big milestone in my life. Since then I have been grateful for its protection. It becomes very aggressive towards anyone who tries to control or limit me, even if I am unaware of their intentions.

When you find your power animal in non-ordinary reality you will either know it or it will communicate to you in some way. You can speak to it if you wish. On returning from your journey it will come back through the tunnel with you so that its energy will be with you at all times, to use or not to use as you choose.

Further Lower World journeys could be undertaken to learn more about your power and how to work effectively with it; to search for a particular power you may need to face a difficult or challenging situation in your life, or possibly to seek healing for yourself. Take the time before journeying to be quite clear in and sure of your intention – I cannot stress often enough this is the key to all successful shamanic work.

UPPER WORLD

How to journey to the Upper World or fifth world is something few teachers seem to feel either qualified or able to teach. Perhaps this is because it is at this level that you meet your true teacher – your own higher self. This is the part of yourself that has guided you into and through, as far as you have allowed it to, your present life. It is the sum of all you have been and learnt in previous lives, and it is not bound by time or space, as are the other levels of yourself. Perhaps it seems to you to be a coincidence that you happen to be reading this book at this time. If the teachings contained in this book seem particularly relevant or appropriate to you at this point in your life then, make no mistake, it was your higher self that guided you here in order to help you with the next step in your personal evolution. If, looking back over your life, you are able to see, as many people can, that there has been a reason and pattern to all the events that have led up to this moment, then know that the hand that has been upon the rudder in your journey through life is that of your own higher self. There is a part of you that knows precisely what you are doing here and where you are going. You can either work cooperatively with that part of your self or you can resist it. If you resist you will find that fighting against the current of your life can be a difficult and punishing business.

Now is the time consciously to meet this part of yourself. The qualities of your higher self, or teacher, are those which you have looked for in parents and life partners. If you have never been totally satisfied with any relationship in your life it is because you were looking for something that nobody else can give you. You were looking for the missing part of yourself – your soul. Meeting this part of yourself now, learning from it, loving it and being loved by it, and finally integrating it into your life will fulfil you in a way no earthly relationship can. Surprisingly, though, as you find more and more joy and fulfilment in this way you will also find that your relationships with others, relieved of your search for the unattainable, will also deepen and take on a new dimension.

Prepare yourself for Upper World journeying in the same way as you did for Lower World journeying. Use whichever method suits you best. You will need to find, in your special place that you start your journeys from, some way by which you can travel upwards: a tree, a mountain, even a ladder will do. The *intention* for your first Upper World journey, as with the Lower World, should be to visit the Upper World to observe.

When the drumming starts, if your intention is clear

in your mind you should begin to travel upwards. Maybe you will need to jump from the top of your tree or if you have a power animal that can fly perhaps you will have help. Whatever happens it is within your power to reach the Upper World. Once you have passed through the gateway to the fifth world, which is equivalent to your crown chakra, have a look around and then return the same way that you arrived.

Repeat this first journey as many times as necessary until you are confident in your ability to reach the Upper World.

You may, reading through this text before journeying, be tempted to try an Upper World journey before the suggested Lower World journeys. I would urge you not to do this, but to work in the order suggested here. Many people find they need to draw consciously on their power in order to reach the upper world. In other words they need the aid of their power animals in this type of journeying. In working at this level of your being it is necessary to have a firm foundation at every other level. That is why we spend the first twenty-one years of our lives building up a healthy physical, emotional and mental energy body. Take just a little time now to become aware of these levels of yourself as fully as possible, and to balance and heal them as necessary, so that your development does not become 'top-heavy' and all your work count for nothing because it did not have sufficient support at your lower levels.

The *intention* for your second Upper World journey will be 'to journey to the Upper World to meet your teacher or higher self'. As stated previously, your higher self is neither (and yet both) male or female, but will present itself to you in a form that you will be able to accept. If, in your search for your teacher, you should come across other beings, you can talk to them and either ask for direction to your teacher or tell them to go away if you feel they are hostile to you.

Do not be discouraged if you do not meet your teacher immediately. They are most definitely there. Sometimes one has much to learn from the search. Once you have met your higher self you will have access to soul level teachings and insights into every aspect of your life, although interpreting these teachings in such a way that your mind self can understand them is a skill that will take a while to develop.

Never lose sight of the fact that you have chosen to live in ordinary reality for a reason. Your ability to move and learn in non-ordinary reality should strengthen and help you in your life's purpose, but it should never be used as an escape from everyday life. With the guidance of your higher self your personal growth and development will speed up immensely. You may well find that you are still guided towards earthly teachers who will work in harmony with your higher self in helping you along the path that you have chosen to walk upon. You may also still have many difficult and perhaps painful situations to face in your life, but with the deeper understanding that your shamanic work will give you, and the ability to work consciously and harmoniously with your own powers, you will find that you will be able to face these situations as the opportunities for growth and learning that they truly are.

In working through the next part of this book, an exploration of and journey around the circle, your higher self will be your main guide. Use the text as a basic map only. Even if you have not yet made direct contact with this part of yourself in your journeying, begin now to attempt to live your life from this level of your being. Be open to its guidance in every area of your life.

Chapter 4
THE CIRCLE

You have noticed that everything an Indian does is in a circle, and that is because the Power of the World always works in circles, and everything tries to be round. In the old days when we were a strong and happy people, all our power came to us from the sacred hoop of the nation and so long as the hoop was unbroken the people flourished. The flowering tree was the living centre of the hoop, and the circle of the four quarters nourished it. The east gave peace and light, the south gave warmth, the west gave rain, and the north with its mighty wind gave strength and endurance. This knowledge came to us from the outer world with our religion. Everything the Power of the World does is done in a circle. The sky is round and I have heard that the earth is round like a ball and so are all the stars. The Wind, in its greatest power, whirls. Birds make their nests in circles, for theirs is the same religion as ours. The sun comes forth and goes down again in a circle. The moon does the same, and both are round.

Even the seasons form a great circle in their changing, and always come back again to where they were. The life of a man is a circle from childhood to childhood and so it is in everything where power moves. Our tipis* were round like the nests of

* tepees

birds and these were always set in a circle, the nation's hoop, a nest of many nests where the Great Spirit meant for us to hatch our children.

Hehaka Sapa (Black Elk), a holy man of the Oglala division of the Teton Dakota Sioux. From **Black Elk Speaks,** *John G. Neihardt (Hutchinson).*

The time has come to explore the Serpent from a different perspective. Imagine you are looking down from above upon the spirals of your own Serpent. It would appear as a circle, which is the universal symbol of wholeness and balance. Several lifetimes could be profitably spent exploring the circle with all its intrinsic wisdom and healing power. What follows is an attempt to open the channels to access your own inner teachings on this subject and also help you to become aware of the direction in which more learning may be possible.

All ancient cultures used the circle not simply as a symbol, but rather as a map to help them understand and relate both to the world around them, and also to themselves. It must be pointed out right away that any workable map is a personal thing. Even given that we are all aiming for the same goal we are all coming at it from our own unique starting points and so some of us will need to travel in totally different directions eventually to reach the same place. On our journey through life, or Earth Walk, we usually either draw to ourselves, or are drawn to, people whose paths are similar to our own. Ancient cultures and religions all grew from the association of people with a similar perspective on life and, in most cases, sadly, an intolerance for anyone with a different perspective from their own.

If you have progressed thus far with this book I think I can safely assume that the direction in which you are travelling is sufficiently similar to my own for what follows to be of benefit to you in exploring your own circle. Do not simply accept what is stated here. The circle you stand in is unique and the way you relate to it, and through it to the world around you, is also entirely your own. More will be said of this later, but do not hesitate to test out what is stated here and reject it if necessary, not as untrue, but simply as incomparable with your own map. A useful analogy here would be to compare the goal we are all aiming at (call it total awareness, balance and harmony, Nirvana, Heaven or what you will) to Paris. A map that would aid me in my journey from the north of England to Paris would also be useful, with a few adaptations, for a person travelling from any other part of the British Isles. But for someone travelling from, say, Australia, my map would be worse than useless. This is not to say that my map, or my truth, would be wrong, just totally irrelevant to them for the journey they would be making.

We have so far been exploring a rather abstract picture or concept of ourselves as the Serpent. We will now try to experience ourselves in a more personal way, working from the inside out, rather than as we did in the first chapter, from the outside in. As you will remember, Spirit, the highest form of energy, condensed itself down into soul energy, then mental energy, working down through emotional and physical energy until it was able to manifest itself as matter (or *mater* – mother) energy on the Earth as our own mineral level of being. Therefore, if we turn the Serpent around and look at it either from above or below it will look something like the diagram opposite.

This is a picture of our own circle. It is something as human beings that we all have in common. The balance of the different levels, how we relate to them and how we reach out through them is uniquely our own. We all are part, though, of other circles: the circle of the Earth, the sun, the stars, moon and planets; the cycles of the seasons, of birth, life, death, resting and then new life; dawn, daytime, dusk and night. All of these circles and many others affect who and what we are very deeply, and must therefore be incorporated, in some way, into our own circle. How we do this depends both on who we are, what qualities we are bringing to the Earth through our female ray, and what we are here to learn and take back with us through the male ray. We will commence our exploration of the circle, then, by examining more closely our connection with the Earth.

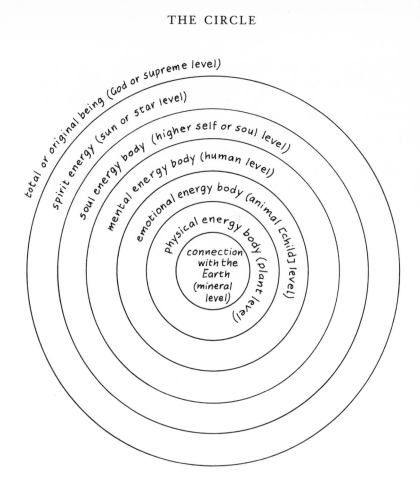

total or original being (God or supreme level)

spirit energy (sun or star level)

soul energy body (higher self or soul level)

mental energy body (human level)

emotional energy body (animal [child] level)

physical energy body (plant level)

connection with the Earth (mineral level)

The Earth

In the above diagram our mineral level, or our connection with the Earth, is at the centre of our circle and many traditions, when constructing two-dimensional medicine wheels (simply a name for a representation of our circle), place it so. Be aware, though, that we are not two-dimensional beings. We exist physically in four dimensions: length, width, height and time. Therefore, our personal circle is, in truth, a sphere that will change as we progress along our life's path. In order to simplify things a little we will fix the point in time at which we wish to explore our circle as now. However, as it is more accurate and, in the long run, easier to understand, we will work with a three-dimensional circle, that is a sphere. For reasons that should be obvious we relate to our mineral level, that is the Earth, as coming from below or beneath.

We have so far examined our relationship to the Earth, concentrating on her role as a loving, caring mother who nourishes us with her own body, and whom we should honour and love for the duration of our earthly lives. It is now time that we learnt to relate to a rather different aspect of the Earth, an aspect that has often been looked upon as rather frightening and threatening. It is what is sometimes referred to as her dark aspect. By learning to understand this aspect of the Earth, and how to work knowingly and harmoniously with it, rather than fearing it and trying to hide from it, which can only lead to imbalance, we can learn more about ourselves and how to work positively with our own 'dark sides'. Eventually we will come to the understanding that both light and dark are but two different aspects of the same thing, and our true nature holds both in balance.

Christians have adapted a Norse name, Hell, from the Norse goddess Hel(a), as the name for the epitome of all evil or, to be more precise, the destination of all evil. Hela is an aspect of the Earth Mother. In Norse mythology she has a body that is half that of a beautiful young woman and half that of a decaying corpse. She rules the Underworld. She is the aspect of the Earth which claims back as her own our physical bodies when we no longer need them. She accepts, in fact she demands, the bodies of all, good and bad, young and old, with equanimity. She also claims all aspects of our earthly lives which we are either not able or willing to refine up to the level of our souls. What did you think happened to all the pain and negative energy that you create (and we all do) as a result of 'mistakes' and experiences which, for one reason or another, you were unable to accept and so fought against? Do not hold on to your own pain and negativity, do not hoard it, or else it will fester and grow within you. It is not enough either simply to ignore it and try to carry on regardless. The Earth Mother claims all your pain and negativity (however shameful and unpleasant) as her own. This is spiritual ecology. Just as Mother Earth will take your physical body when it is returned to her (and the physical waste of all life forms), rot or compost it down and transform it into good nourishing soil from which other beings may draw life and sustenance, so will she take all other forms of what we may consider waste, or negativity, from us, compost them down and then return them to her children as positive energies for their use.

This cycle of energy exchange forms the basis of spiritual ecology, and the health and harmony of all things, on all levels, depends upon it. As humankind deliberately flouts these basic laws, on all levels of their existence, we see the growing imbalance in ourselves and the world around us. As with all shamanic work we must look initially to rebalance this disharmony within ourselves and the sphere of our own personal lives before we can radiate out healing and balance around us.

On the most basic level this could mean considering how your household generates and disposes of its waste. It is just not possible to be spiritually 'pure' or 'advanced' if you are physically polluting and poisoning the body of our Mother Earth. With the combination of a little thought and care you will soon see opportunities for helping rather than harming the Earth in all areas of your life. The rapid growth in 'environmentally friendly' products and recycling facilities are all steps in the right direction.

Looking, though, beyond the physical, what do you do with your emotional and mental waste? If you feel anger, pain, hate or despair towards or because of anyone or anything, or any incident or situation, what do you do about it? Ignoring it, or pretending it isn't happening, won't work. Nor will trying not to feel as you do if the situation genuinely requires a negative response. If, however, you deliberately feed your emotional waste to the Earth, so that it can be transformed into positive, beneficial energy, then you are actively helping both the situation and yourself.

Thoughts have both form and substance. Negative or destructive thoughts do not cease to be because you do not act upon them or because you refuse to acknowledge that you occasionally have them (for we all do), although the less energy you put into them the weaker they will be. They become trapped negative energy, either in your own mental energy body, or if you are able to release them it could even be possible for others to connect to them and possibly act upon them, so giving them energy and form on other levels.

Perhaps you are beginning to see how important it is to be able to recognise and return deliberately to the Earth any negativity that you generate – and you will generate some, however well meaning you may be, just as you generate physical waste simply by the process of living in your body. It is also important to be able to recognise and know how to cope with any negative energies from another source which either accidentally or deliberately come your way.

PSYCHIC ATTACK

We are now approaching a subject which is often described as psychic attack. This term is used in many different contexts to describe many quite different situations. I use it here to describe a situation where someone is deliberately (although sometimes unknowingly) aiming negative mental or emotional energy at you (as opposed to physical attack which, of course, involves negative physical energy). Most books and teachers of this subject will give you techniques for either reflecting these bad energies back to their source or else barricading yourself against them in some way so that they cannot reach and harm you. This is not my way. It is not that these techniques will not work, it is just that they do not solve anything. Reflecting negativity back to its source is not only going against the natural spiritual ecology cycle, but it is also doing further harm to a person who, in all probability, is trapped by their own negativity and is in great need of help.

Similarly, simply blocking yourself against negativity from an outside source can be seen at best as a neutral act, and you are certainly not helping the situation by leaving negative energy at large in the environment where it has the potential of doing great harm. I am certainly not suggesting that as an altruistic act you should open yourself up to all the negative energies that you may come in contact with, although there are methods, which require many years of work, by which you can create a channel within yourself through which negativity can be earthed, rather like a lightening conductor. Do not attempt any such thing without the direct instruction of either your own higher self or an experienced shamanic teacher. The dangers of not being able to rid yourself of the negativity you take in are very real.

RETURNING NEGATIVE ENERGIES
TO THE EARTH

The following two methods can be used to earth either your own negativity or that coming to you from an outside source. Method one is for earthing negativity that is known and that you are ready to let go of, such as anger over a particular incident or pain over a finished relationship. Method two is more suited to an ongoing situation such as jealousy in a current relationship or anger about events over which you have no control.

You should, hopefully, by now have established a close working relationship with your higher self. So, before trying either of these methods check them out with your own teacher to see which would be best suited to your particular needs and if there are any personal adaptations of either which would make them work better for you. If you do not yet have that close a relationship with your higher self be assured, nevertheless, that your higher self is there guiding you, and try to be as aware of and receptive to that guidance as possible.

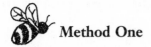 **Method One**

You will need a stone, rock or fairly large pebble that you have found for yourself in a natural environment. If it has passed through anyone else's hands you will need to cleanse it by holding it under running water for a few minutes with the clear *intention* that it should be cleansed.

Make whatever preparations you normally make before commencing any shamanic work. When you are relaxed, quiet in body and mind, and ready to begin, pick up your stone. Hold it in your hand before you and begin to tell it, either aloud or silently, all about the negative energies that you wish to be rid of. Explain clearly the whole situation which has led up to this moment. You may well find as you do so that you gain new insights into your problem and its relevance to your life. When you feel that you have said all there is to say and you are ready completely to let go of your pain, fear or whatever, then take a deep breath, bring the stone to your mouth and breathe out all your negativity into the stone. You may need to repeat this several times until you are sure that it has all gone.

Because, as explained previously, minerals are holders of energy, just as your own mineral level is that by which you are held on the Earth in material existence, the stone that you have chosen (and which will also have chosen you) will be able to take the negative energy which you are releasing and hold it.

The next step is to return your stone to the Earth so that the negative energy that it is holding can be composted down and transformed into positive energy. This can be done by either throwing it into the sea or a river or stream, or else burying it in the Earth. Whichever you choose should be done with the clear *intention* of returning your negativity to the Earth so that it can be transformed. This should be done in a reverent manner to show gratitude to the mineral kingdom which is help-ing you in this way.

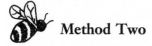 **Method Two**

To deal with negativity which, for one reason or another you are not able to completely release in one go, a rather different approach is needed.

A mineral sample will be used in this method also. I use black tourmaline for this purpose, but choose what-ever seems right for you.

Prepare yourself in the usual way for shamanic work. When you are ready, as in method one, take up your rock or stone and explain the situation which is causing you to take this action as fully as you can. Now take the stone and bury it in the Earth, marking the place so it can later be retrieved. Your intention in doing this is to create a channel through which all negativity engendered by the situation which you have connected the stone to, can be earthed, and so transformed. This channel will exist for as long as the stone remains buried, although it can be strengthened from time to time by retrieving and cleansing it, and then repeating the above process.

When the need for the channel has passed your stone can be retrieved, thoroughly cleansed and used again. A stone used frequently for this work can become a power-ful channel through which negativity can be earthed, and a very useful and valued helper.

This method can also be used to help and heal others, even those to whom you could not explain your shamanic work. It is important to understand, though, that help or healing is not something which can be forced on someone. All that you can do, by working in the same way as you would for yourself, is to create a channel by which their problems, pain or whatever, can be returned to the Earth if they are willing to release them. If, for some reason, a person is holding on to their negativity then there is, sadly, nothing you can or should do to force them to release it. That step is for them to take in their own way and in their own time.

We have now, hopefully, a stronger and more balanced connection to, and understanding of our Mother the Earth. As she turns and spirals in her own perpetual dance about the sun we should be beginning to be aware of where our own circle touches hers, and how our own spiral dance of life blends in and harmonises with hers.

It is now time to step beyond our mineral level of being and explore our physical energy in relation to our own circle.

The West

Your physical energy body surrounds you. It is an integral part of you. But how you relate to it, what you use it for and what you allow to work through it gives it a uniqueness, or a direction, all of its own. Different teachers, from different traditions, will show you different orientations for this aspect of your self, but only you can really know what is right for you.

Why are you living in a physical body at this time? Why are you living in that particular body? These are not questions to be skimmed over, but to be pondered deeply. As you worked through the tasks given in Chapter 1 you may well have already found part of your answer. I strongly suggest that these questions should be the subject of several shamanic journeys and that you should not proceed further until you have at least tried to find answers to them.

I think you will eventually find that your answers fall into two categories. The first category being things that you have to give while on the Earth (related to your female ray) and the second being things that you have to gather while on the Earth, such as experience and learning (related to your male ray). Both of these can be summed up by one word: *change*. You are living in a body so that change or transformation can take place both through you and to you. Hopefully you have some idea of what changes you are capable of working and that you are personally needing, but always be prepared for surprises!

GETTING TO KNOW THE SPIRIT KEEPERS

In the circle of the day, which represents one turn of the Earth, there are two times of change: dawn and dusk, which are ascribed to the directions of the east and the west because of the position of the rising and setting sun, or the way in which spirit relates to matter at that point in time. Also in the circle of the year, which represents one circuit of the Earth around the Sun, there are two times of transition: the spring when energy is moving outward – a time of birth, growth and beginnings; and the autumn, when the opposite is happening, and things are being condensed and pulled down deep into themselves, plant energies are being stored in their roots and seeds, and in the animal kingdom it is also the time of death or dormancy. Because of the relationship between spirit and matter at these times spring is seen as belonging to the east, and autumn to the west.

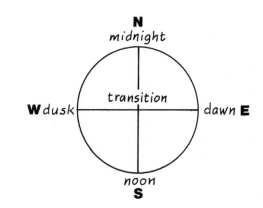

Circle of the day

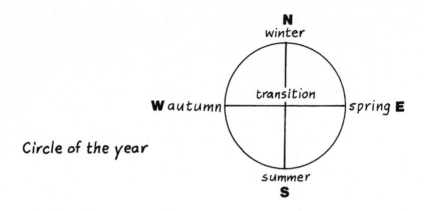

Circle of the year

On many Native American medicine wheels, although by no means all, physical life is seen as belonging in the west. When talking about the west in this context we are not simply talking about a physical direction, but rather the archetypal qualities connected to that direction. The qualities that energy has when it approaches the Earth from the east are those of quickening, awakening and enlightenment, as can be seen at dawn and in the spring. The qualities energy has when appoaching the Earth from the west are those of slowing, condensing, drawing in and, as said before, transforming.

These qualities cannot really be learnt from a book. It is necessary for you to relate to them directly. This, though, is not something which can be done in a few days or weeks. Just as a relationship with another person takes time to build up and understand so will your relationship with the archetypal energies, or the spirit keepers of the four directions. A very basic start can be made by finding a space in your day to sit quietly and sketch a circle as shown, dividing it into four, and ascribing each quarter to a direction. Now think of anything

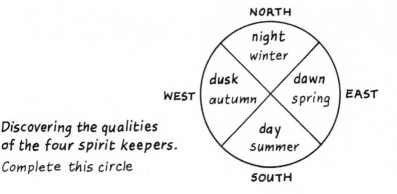

Discovering the qualities
of the four spirit keepers.
Complete this circle

you like, and try and fit it on to the circle in the appropriate place. The seasons and times of the day have already
been done for you, but you could still investigate the
qualities associated with these. The phases of the moon
would be an obvious subject, as would the life cycle of a
plant, or animal, or even a human being.

Gradually you will come to understand not just the
qualities associated with the four directions, but also
what they mean to you and how you relate to them.
Eventually you will be able to choose how to relate to
them, and take another step towards harmonising and
healing yourself and the world around you.

If it feels right to you, as it does to me, to connect to the wisdom
and energies of the west through your physical energy body then
what follows will be of use to you. If, for any reason, a different
orientation seems more appropriate to you then the following
may well still be of some interest and help.

To connect to and experience the character of
the energy of the west try standing outside facing the
west on a clear, sunny day, what do you see? What do
you experience? Early in the day your face will be shaded

and your shadow will be before you, long and thin. You will feel the warmth of the sun on your back, and you may well long to turn around and face it, but the beginning of the day is behind you. The day will have passed its mid-point before you can see the sun, feel its warmth and energy on your face, and greet it directly. Now your shadow is behind you. You are facing the direction that the sun is travelling in. Your energy is moving in harmony with that of your Spirit Father – from east to west – towards the point when, in a blaze of glory, or with a quiet, gradual fading, the sun is gone.

Was that the future? Was that what the course of the day was all about? Was everything working towards and leading up to the departure of the sun – darkness, coldness and death? What is your life about, as the spirit that flows through you follows that same inescapable path from east to west, birth to death?

UNDERSTANDING DEATH

When a child is born the only thing that we can be sure that its future holds is death, yet that is probably the thing that it will be most shielded from and least prepared for. What is the fear and mystery that surrounds death all about? Could it possibly be that our modern, linear way of thinking sees death as the edge of a precipice, total oblivion, rather than as everything in the natural world tells us it must be, a point on a circle, part of a cycle that we will repeat time and time again, a transition rather than an ending.

Even your physical body which, in its inability to serve you indefinitely, is the cause of your death has its own kind of immortality. As Einstein tells us matter can be neither destroyed nor created, only changed. The very atoms (units of physical energy) of which your present body is comprised may once have been part of the body of a dinosaur or a tree in some primaeval forest. As when we were learning to return negativity to the Earth for it to be transformed into positive energy, we find that there is no such thing as an ending, no such thing as death, only transformation.

This is too big a concept really to accept immediately. So look back now over your life at all the 'little deaths' you have suffered. All the endings and the losses, the painful and the happy changes of your life. It would be a good idea to list them. Now, taking your time, try to examine each of these 'little deaths' in this new way, as a transformation, rather than an ending. What was being transformed into what? Did you welcome the change or did you fight against it? Was the change successful or not? Is it possible that you have had a series of 'little deaths' all trying to work the same transformation, but which you, for whatever reason, have blocked?

This exercise may take weeks or even months, but I think you will eventually recognise the fact that if you accept and work positively with whatever transformation is happening to you it will happen much faster and less painfully than if you fear and resist it. Acknowledging the fact that you are in a physical body for the purpose of experiencing change and transformation can help enormously with this. Once these 'little deaths' and, in truth, also the greater death at the end of your present physical life can be seen in the light of the learning and growing experiences that you need they lose their horror and power to engender fear. Although they may still involve suffering you will find you accept and even welcome it in the way that a pregnant woman welcomes the labour pains that end her pregnancy and bring her child into the world. For birth and death are but different perspectives of the same thing, just as the sunset in one place is the moment of sunrise in another and, as you experience autumn, people in the opposite hemisphere of the Earth are greeting the spring.

The South

It would seem that the way you relate to the energies of the south and the north would depend upon which hemisphere you live in, but this is not strictly so. Look at climbing plants that originated in the Northern hemisphere, such as honeysuckle, and you will see that they climb by wrapping themselves around their supports in a clockwise, or sun-wise, direction, whereas plants that were originally indigenous to the southern hemisphere, such as runner beans, regardless of where they are now growing, twine around their supports in an anti-clockwise direction.

Which is the natural direction that your energy moves in? Are you left or right handed? Does your dominant hand correspond to your dominant eye and foot? We are really exploring here what could be described as your own polarity. As stated earlier your energy moves rhythmically and spirally. Understanding the direction of your spiral can help you orient yourself within your own circle.

As a guide your dominant hand is controlled by your male, or yang, ray or aspect and your other hand, usually considered to be your passive or receptive hand, is controlled by your female ray. This, however, is not always a true guide because of various cultural superstitions and taboos which can lead to adults interfering with the natural polarity of a child before it is aware of what is happening, leading to possible lifelong energy imbalance and disharmony.

In the Western magical tradition clockwise is called dieseil and anti-clockwise widdershins. Because of an awareness of the natural energy patterns in this part of the world (the northern hemisphere) dieseil was considered good and wholesome, whereas widdershins was thought to be a sign of bad luck. This understanding was used in what was described as black magic to create disharmony or in white magic to heal and harmonise. With this knowledge, but not the understanding to go with it, right-handed people were accepted as their energy patterns conformed to the normal dieseil pattern, and left-handed people were persecuted and, in some cases, even killed because their energy flowed in a widdershins spiral and they were so considered evil. Even quite recently children in schools were made to write right-handed, regardless of their natural inclinations.

This, quite obviously, is a misinterpretation of a basic fact. Although dieseil is the natural spiralic pattern for energy to follow in the northern hemisphere, widdershins is also a naturally occurring energy pattern usually found in the southern hemisphere. Your own polarity, whatever it may be, is the correct and most natural way for your energy to express itself. By being aware of it and working in harmony with it, not only can you live in the most effective way for you personally, you can also increase your understanding of how you relate to the world around you and your knowledge of your own circle.

 CHECKING YOUR POLARITY

You will need your pendulum.

Prepare yourself as you normally do for shamanic work. When you are ready take up your pendulum in whichever hand feels right. Hold it on a short thread of about 3 to 4 in (75 to 100 cm). You are going to communicate with your instinctive animal self. Ask to be shown in which direction your energy naturally flows. Your pendulum should start to move in the same direction as your energy. I always feel it is best to check this several times. If you have a friend who is sufficiently experienced in shamanic work to be able to check this for you, without getting confused about whose energy they are tuning into then that is also a good idea.

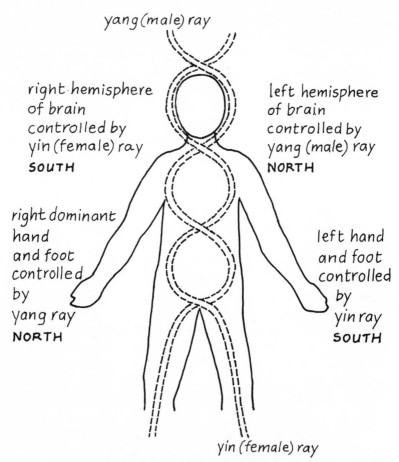

yang (male) ray

right hemisphere
of brain
controlled by
yin (female) ray
SOUTH

left hemisphere
of brain
controlled by
yang (male) ray
NORTH

right dominant
hand
and foot
controlled
by
yang ray
NORTH

left hand
and foot
controlled
by
yin ray
SOUTH

yin (female) ray

Polarity of a right-handed person

A clockwise movement would indicate that you are naturally right handed. An anti-clockwise movement would indicate that you are naturally left handed. If no clear answer is forthcoming this would indicate that either you are totally ambidextrous and your energies are in perfect balance or, as is more likely, your energies are in such conflict with their natural pattern having been denied them that it is not possible to detect any clear direction. If this is the case you should try to contact parents, or teachers and friends who knew you as a child, and find out whether you were naturally left handed, but taught to use your right hand instead. If this is the case then the only course by which you will be able to rebalance your polarity will be one of re-education. Slowly, devoting at first perhaps only a few minutes a day you will have to give your left hand a chance to learn all the skills that were denied it all that time ago, and gradually it will re-establish its dominance and your natural energy pattern will once more be established.

You may find that your natural energy pattern has been interfered with during your childhood but it is not causing you too many problems. For instance, the pendulum may show that your energy naturally flows anti-clockwise, but you have been taught to write with your right hand. It may not be worth you embarking on a programme of re-education. You would probably find it very easy to write with your left hand as your energy pattern is still clear and it has retained its dominance, but simply being aware of your polarity may be quite sufficient for you.

As the polarity diagram shows your yin or female energies can be described as your southern polarity and your dominant yang ray as your northern polarity. In the northern hemisphere, when energy approaches from the south, it is usually warm and nurturing, bringing with it qualities of openness and growth. The south is connected with summer and the middle part of the day when the sun is strongest, so it also has the quality of strength.

If you stand with your back to the east so that you are aligned to the natural path of life, whereby everything flows from birth to death (and so back to birth again) as we have already seen, you will find that the south is to your left: the side of your body on which, if you are right handed, your yin ray dominates your hand and foot – the parts of yourself with which you reach out to the world around you and your energies align to those of the world around you. If you are left handed, or your energy naturally flows anti-clockwise, your yin ray connects to the south through your mind and your physical energy body. I leave you to explore the implications of this for yourself. Look not only at your own body, its balance, health and how you use it to relate to the world around you, but also on a grander scale at different cultural characteristics of both people and nations. Naturally, for a person living in the southern hemisphere this would be reversed. For someone whose lifestyle leads to them frequently crossing the equator it would help enormously for them to be aware of their own polarity, and how the connection between that and the polarity of the Earth changes according to where they are on the Earth.

LETTING GO OF FEAR

The wisdom of the traditional medicine wheel that I work with relates through the south, the direction of growth, openness, learning and strength, to the animal or child level of our being, the emotional energy centre. The south, connected as it is to summer in the northern hemisphere, can be related to the time of a person's life between birth and death when he or she should be learning and growing. The childlike qualities of openness and innocence which are so necessary for true learning and growth to take place, and which are all too rarely retained nowadays, even throughout childhood, have been recognised by many spiritual teachers as the key to what Christ called the kingdom of heaven – perhaps a term which could be used to describe the successful completion of our life on Earth.

Why do we close doors and erect barriers? Without nourishment we cannot grow on any level of our being. Yet many of us find it impossible to accept much of the nourishment that is freely offered to us. Of course we need to be discerning. We cannot simply accept everything we are told or given. But neither do children! A child is able to be innocent and open because a child trusts. It trusts its parents and teachers to care for it. It trusts to its own purity of intent to attract to it things of an equally high order. It trusts its own higher self to guide it into life in the way best suited for its particular needs.

When you were a child you were open and innocent. You trusted implicitly until your trust was betrayed. By whom or what was your trust betrayed? Was it people or life in general? And what have you replaced that trust with? You have replaced it with fear.

Fear is the reason that you cannot fully participate in life. Fear is the reason that you cannot totally open yourself to the learning experiences towards which your higher self guides you, with such loving patience. Your fear is stunting your growth. You must learn to reach through it to connect totally to the power of the south and to balance your own emotional energy.

As when you were working with the west and coming to understand death I want you now to look back into your past. Starting with your earliest childhood memories list down each betrayal, each occasion when the world or the people around you let you down and betrayed your trust in them. We are working now with your emotional energy centre, the level of your inner child, so you may well find that the use of a pendulum as described in Chapter 1 will aid you in this. Do not rush. These memories will probably be very painful to you and so will have been repressed. It will take time for you to reach them. Deal with any negativity which results from them as you have been taught.

If you come across any memory blocks which it is not possible for you to break through on your own then I suggest you seek the help of an experienced shamanic healer. There could be several reasons for these blocks which are beyond the scope of this book, but it is likely that you could be helped by one of several soul therapy techniques which only a trained and experienced healer would be able to offer you.

Once you have a list, even if it is not complete, you can begin to examine each occasion in turn. It may well be that seeing the situation anew from the viewpoint of an adult you realise that there was no betrayal at all, simply a misunderstanding. But it will certainly be true in many cases that the betrayal was all too real. You will need to examine these cases very closely. Why were you let down and betrayed in such a way? I think you will eventually see that everything that happened to you happened as a result of disharmony and imbalance in the people and situation around you. People who are unable to heal and harmonise themselves cannot help but spread disharmony and dis-ease around them. They need help. Surely this is the work you are at present engaged in. As we have seen, as we realise and harmonise ourselves, we are healing and balancing the world around us. We cannot do this if we take on the problems of others. If we do that we are simply multiplying problems rather than resolving them.

Taking each case in turn you must come to understand and forgive the people or situations which hurt you. For you cannot help or heal anyone or anything if you blame or resent them. Nor can you help yourself if you hold on to your fear. I think you will come to realise that your betrayal was the inevitable culmination of a long line of betrayals, and the people involved acted and reacted in the only way that they at that time were able. Now that you can see this you will be able to break the pattern. Earth your negativity as you have learnt and you will find that your fear goes with it. Once you understand you will no longer fear. Gradually you will regain your trust and openness. Your child self will be all the more beautiful now that it is working in love, harmony and balance with all the other levels of yourself. Your connection to the south will be strengthened as you find you are open to the growth and learning that you came to the Earth for.

The North

Understanding your own polarity, take what follows as a guide only and relate to it in whatever way is right for you.

Standing again with your back to the east you will find that your right hand is towards the north. If you are right handed then this is the part of you which you reach out to the world with in order to give and do. The world we live in is shaped by our right hands as the tools of our minds and it is through the north that I choose to work with the mental energy centre.

In the circle of the year the north can be related to winter time when nothing is growing and there seems to be a pause or breathing space in the natural world. For us this can be seen as a time of taking stock or of consolidation. A pause for thought perhaps. But what are thoughts? Do they have any substance, any reality? Where do they come from? Where do they go? What controls them or, perhaps, what do they control?

Close your eyes. Think of yourself ten years ago. What did you look like? What were you doing? Concentrate hard until you can build up a picture of yourself as you were then and the life you were leading at that time; until you can be back there with that earlier version of yourself in your reality of ten years ago.

Now, still with your eyes closed project yourself ten years into the future. Where will you be in ten years' time? See yourself in whatever future you choose. Whom will you be with? What will you look like? Continue until you have built up a clear picture of the future that you, as you are at the moment, choose for yourself.

Now open your eyes. What have you just done apart from indulging in what is commonly called day-dreaming? You have just proved that thoughts are not bound by time. You are able to time travel. Perhaps the future that you chose to visit is not the one with ten years' more experience of life and choices made along the way, that you will end up at in ten years' time. But it is still a valid future. Perhaps your vision of it is so strong that nothing more can influence you on the subject and you will be able to earth your thought energy in such a way as to create your own reality.

Thoughts are not bound by time. Nor are they bound by any of the other dimensions of the material world. Unlike your emotions, which are dependent on either the world around you, or the other levels of your being, needing something to react to, your thoughts are totally free and creative. At least they have the potential to be so. Freeing, healing and balancing the lower levels of your being should already have gone a long way towards freeing your own inherent creativity.

Jewish–Christian myth tells us that people are made in the image of the creator. We are therefore also creators. Although animals build they do so according to the ancient instinctive and learnt wisdom of their kind. Your creativity is your uniquely human ability. Cold abstract thought robbed of its spark of creativity becomes lifeless and inhuman, just as people need fire to survive the cold of the winter. The difference between wisdom and knowledge is that wisdom takes knowledge one step further, it applies it and so is a creative living thing, whereas knowledge without a use or application is a useless dead weight in our minds.

CREATING YOUR OWN REALITY

Native American myth tells us that this world is but a thought in the mind of Wankan Tanka, the great spirit. We have seen how spirit energy condenses down to create soul, then mental, then emotional, then physical energy and material reality. The physical world that surrounds you and all the trappings of your life here on the earth were once thought energy. This creative thought energy was activated in the correct way, either intentionally or unintentionally, to condense it down into the denser energies of emotion, the physical and matter.

Thought energy is being transformed into material reality all the time, usually unconsciously. Look around you, it is possible you will find that many of the trappings of your life, your home, your job, your family even, started out as ideas, thoughts in your mind with no reality beyond that. So perhaps you already know how to earth your thoughts in such a way as to give them reality on another level. How did it happen? Did you have to work very hard at it or was it just luck?

Thought energy has to be strong enough to condense down and it also has to be activated in the right way. There is no need, though, for sessions of deep concentration to project energy into your vision of how the future should be. You know enough now about how energy moves, especially your own energy, to be able to bring your thoughts into harmony with the rest of your being and utilise all the energy that flows through you to strengthen your thoughts. Harmony really is the key. Practitioners of sorcery and black magic have a much harder time of things than they need have. It is far harder to manipulate and control than it is to work in harmony and cooperative love with the world around you. Look at how easily a bird flies in the air, riding the air currents, instinctively knowing how to work with the natural energies of the air, yet still able to steer a course through them and choose its own direction. Now look at all the energy that humankind expends in their attempts to conquer the air. All right, so humankind also usually gets to the places they wanted to go, but look at the cost both to humankind and the world around them. Choose now whether you wish to fly like a bird or a helicopter. Do you wish to create in harmony with the energy patterns of the natural world and all the beings that you share it with or do you wish to manipulate these energies for your own personal profit? If the latter is your intention then I am afraid that you are reading the wrong book!

It should be clear that only certain types of thoughts can be strengthened by allowing all your life energy to flow through them. Any which are out of harmony with any level of your being will be weakened by this disharmony. For instance, if you are thinking of moving to a different area, but your mineral and plant level know that the place where you are already living is right for you and your health would suffer from a move, then those levels of your self would not only refuse to lend your thoughts their energy, they would, in all likelihood, draw energy from them. This is why it is so important to be aware of all the levels of your being and be prepared to work cooperatively with them. As you already know the only level of yourself that is able to take an overall view in this way is your soul level, so I thoroughly recommend doing an Upper World journey to discuss the full implications of any thoughts you may wish to activate before going any further.

When you are certain that your thoughts are in total harmony with all the levels of your being, how do you get the energy flowing to strengthen them? For this we need to access both our male and female energies, and it is possible to do this through a gateway chakra where they cross. The most convenient one for this purpose is the throat chakra. This is our speech centre and, simply by speaking out, in the form of an affirmation, the thoughts which we wish to strengthen, it is possible to put them in harmonious contact with all our energies. It is important that your affirmation should be positive, for instance: 'I will stop smoking' or 'I will move to the country'; rather than negative such as 'I won't smoke any more' or 'I won't live here any longer'. This should be done on a regular basis at least twice a day for as long as it takes your thoughts to be brought into physical manifestation.

MAKING A PRAYER FEATHER

The next step is to activate your thoughts. To some extent this has already been done. The method I teach of energising them not only acts as a safeguard so that only harmonious thoughts will be able to be energised, but as your thoughts begin to flow with your life energies they will become active within your life. To enhance this further, an adaptation of a traditional Native American tool, a prayer feather, can be used.

The Oxford English Dictionary definition of prayer is 'a solemn request or entreaty'. It can also mean 'giving thanks'. These two different meanings sum up nicely the idea of energy flowing down into matter and then returning back whence it came. It is important to remember that the energy we are using to strengthen our thoughts does not come from the mind, it is being directed by the mind.

With the *intention* of 'directing higher energies by the creative power of your mind in order to activate and earth your thoughts in such a way as to give them reality on other levels' begin your search for a feather. Birds are beings of the air, the element commonly connected with thought and the north. They are also beings which rise above the earth, and so come closer than us to the realms of soul and spirit. In some traditions the soul is thought to take the form of a bird when it leaves the body either in sleep or at death.

Your search for the right feather may take either hours, days or weeks, or you may find that when the time is right your feather will find you. Bear in mind that anything obtained from a bird in fear or pain will probably have energies attached to it that will not aid you in your work. As long as you have not in any way contributed to the creature's suffering, though, the feather can still be used as long as it is smudged thoroughly.

You are going to use your feather to channel the energy needed to activate your thoughts to the Earth. It can be decorated in any way which you feel is appropriate, using substances or colours for example that are connected with the different levels of being you are working with.

When you are ready, go to a place in nature where you can work undisturbed and where you can leave your feather knowing that it is unlikely to be interfered with. Prepare yourself to work in the usual way. Now take up your feather in your right hand (or left if you are left-handed), and speak your affirmation out loud. Continue to do so until you feel the energy that this builds up begin to flow through your feather. This may take some time. Do not worry if your affirmation becomes a chant or a song. You are responding to the vibration of the energy flowing through you and singing a true power song. It may be that the sounds of the words you are speaking will change slightly, because you are making a stronger connection to them which goes beyond your conditioned learning.

When you feel the energy flowing through your feather, press it into the ground so that it stands upright. The higher energies which will activate your thoughts have now been connected to the earth where they will condense into material reality.

You may wish to make a token 'give-away' as a gesture of thanks to the spiritual energies, or the great spirit, that make this happen. I would not recommend the traditional gift of tobacco or herbs, unless they have been grown in your own garden. With modern agricultural methods it is a bit hypocritical to make a gift to the Earth of something which she was plundered to obtain in the first place. A gift of your time to pick up litter or clear away dead undergrowth would be more appropriate, or perhaps some organically grown grain to feed the birds and small mammals in winter.

Your feather must now be left where it is. You may find it inspiring and renewing to visit it from time to time, but it should not be touched. You may find that as time goes by, and you learn and develop more that the vision of the future that you were working towards changes slightly. As long as the energy to create your reality is flowing harmoniously through you, your prayer feather will be acting almost as an aeriel for this energy and will continue to work with your growing vision.

The East

The east, the place of the rising sun, has been revered in many traditions as the direction from which enlightenment comes. Ancient stone circles align to it, and many modern-day religions build altars and bow to it. Not only the sun, but also the moon and stars arise in the east, so it is seen as the place of origins and beginnings. In the Christian story of the birth of Christ the wise men came from the east, and this is a common theme in other traditions, so wisdom is seen as another quality of the east. As we have already experienced, wisdom and spiritual enlightenment can come to us only through our higher selves or souls from whom our earthly selves originated. So, on the medicine wheel, the east is connected to the soul qualities of enlightenment and initiation. Our soul energy body is the one which we try to connect to through the east.

To appreciate this fully rise before dawn on a fine morning and go to a clear, natural place. Seat yourself comfortably on the Earth and become aware of the darkness around you. Feel it envelop you, both comforting and a little frightening. As you welcome it you may experience a profound sense of peace and stillness.

Allow yourself time to achieve this sense of oneness with the dark and stillness of the night. As the dawn approaches you may well feel it as a rising anticipation and excitement well before your eyes are able to detect any sign of an increase in light levels.

As the first rays of light creep over the horizon observe yourself and your surroundings very closely. How does your body feel? Does your awareness of it change in any way as the light begins to fall on it? Are you aware of any changes in temperature or weather conditions that come with the increasing light? How are any plants around you reacting? Be aware of any sounds, smells or sensations that you experience.

Now, what about your feelings? Do you feel exhilarated or depressed? Peaceful or excited? Happy or sad? Does the increasing light affect your emotions in a positive or negative way? If your instincts prompt you to react in any particular way, adopt a special posture or make certain movements then give them free reign. You may even feel it appropriate to sing as the birds will certainly be doing. Are you aware of any other animal life around you and how it is reacting to the dawn?

Observe any stray thoughts or mental images that come into your mind. Be receptive to any sudden insights or understandings that may come to you. Dismiss nothing, but don't try to hold on to it either, merely take note of it and let it continue on its way, perhaps leading you to further and deeper understanding, or perhaps clearing the way for what follows.

You are not participating in any way in the dawn, you are simply observing and experiencing it. When you feel ready it is a good idea to note down all that you were aware of, as small details are easily later overlooked and forgotten. You now have a description of your own personal experience of how soul energy moves in each level of your being and the world around you. Did your body feel warm and tingly, or cold and still as the day dawned?

However it felt is right for you. Watch out for that feeling again, learn to recognise and welcome it, because that is how your body feels when it is experiencing the guidance and direction of your higher self.

As I write this book from my soul level I am able to recognise a certain feeling in my body that assures me that my fingers on the keys of the word processor are under the direct guidance of my higher self and not, as often is the case, the servants of my mind. Learn also to recognise this experience in your emotional energy body and your mental energy body. You may eventually find that you are able directly to tune into your soul energy by deliberately attuning your body, emotions and mind to the pattern that you have learnt to recognise. Then you will truly have begun to be a being of the fifth world where all the other levels of your being are harmonious partners under the loving guidance of your higher self.

Above

The direction from which the source of light or energy comes which illuminates all other directions is of course above. In all traditions spirit is seen as being above matter, either literally or allegorically. Just as life on Earth, without the light and heat of the sun, would not be possible, so without spirit, matter could not exist.

The spiritual being which has prime responsibility for us, and for all life forms both on Earth and in the entire solar system, was referred to by the Native Americans as the Great Spirit. Other traditions, while using different names for this being, and in some cases different names for different aspects of it, still in some form or another, retained a basic understanding of it as a bringer of light and life, and its connection with the sun. From Ahura Mazdao of the ancient Persians, Ra of the ancient Egyptians, Zeus or Apollo of the ancient Greeks and Romans, to the

Christ of the Christians the 'light of the world' and the son (sun?) of god, linked in most of the mystery traditions with the angel Michael who comes from the sun.

A SPIRIT QUEST

If, as our ancestors did, we take the sun as a physical representation of the source of all spirit, what can we learn from it to enhance not only our understanding of true spirituality but also to bring our lives into greater harmony with our own spiritual essence?

Making the acquisition of this learning the purpose behind a further shamanic quest is to be recommended. Choose a day, or even a few days if at all possible, to put aside for this purpose. A bright, sunny day would be ideal, but do not worry if that is not possible. The sun is there at all times, even when it cannot be seen, and perhaps this is a part of what you must learn.

I would urge you to undertake an Upper World shamanic journey to ask your higher self for any guidance or teaching your higher self can give you concerning your quest before laying too many plans. Some people find that greater insights come to them during the same part of the circle of the year as they were born in, as they are then in alignment with the path that their own spiritual ray took as it came into matter. This is certainly not true in all cases, though, and only your own higher self would be in a position to know what would be best for you.

Location also is something which you must take guidance on. Obviously somewhere outside where you are unlikely to be disturbed is essential. But if you are disturbed do not abandon your quest as, whatever form that disturbance takes, it will form a part of the learning which you seek.

If journeying is difficult for you then be assured that your higher self is with you wishing to help and support you all it can, so simply try to open yourself to this help and guidance and act upon it in whatever way seems appropriate.

Perhaps fasting would be right for you, perhaps not. If so and you are in good overall health be sure to take sufficient fluids and not to overdo things. If you are in a secluded enough place and the weather is mild, then perhaps being naked would be right. Just in case you end up in a police station, though, it might be a good idea to have a copy of this book with you to help explain things!

You should be experienced enough in shamanic work by now to be able to open yourself to the teaching that is given to you in whatever form it takes. The following (an extract from a quest of my own) is given simply as an act of sharing. It is in no way meant to guide, replace or surpass your own direct connection with spirit. I wish you joy, success and fulfilment in this highest of quests.

The sun shone on me and the ocean before me. With my eyes closed I looked into its face. It seemed to be the face of a lion. Arms reached out from either side of the face, drawing me to it, holding me in an embrace of infinite warmth, infinite love.

I became aware of my teacher telling me to open my eyes and look at the sea.

I watched the sea for a long time. Days . . . weeks . . . maybe months or years. I saw it in all its different aspects; life giver and destroyer; the serenity of a tranquil day, the terror of the storm; friend, foe, lover, mother, child and master. The beauty of the clouds, each different as they left; the power of the rivers and streams as they returned.

And I saw my life with all its joys and sorrows, hopes and fears. I saw the diversity of all life and I understood that just as the essence of the sea in all its many different aspects is simply water, so the essence of my life, or my spirit is simply *love*, as is the essence of all life.

Just as storms and floods, as well as tranquillity and beauty, are expressions of water so all the different aspects of myself and my life are expressions of love. All of the vast complicated being that each of us is, is simply our own expression of the love that is our essence and that essence reaches out to touch and embrace everything, like the sea.

The Centre

Within your own personal medicine wheel where do you stand? Have you created a circle of your own out of rocks, stones or whatever felt right, or have you stood atop a hill on a clear day and acknowledged the circle of the horizon, looking for markers that others may have left as they understood the circle of their own lives in relationship to the greater circle of life of which they were and still are a part? Trees, rocks and buildings may all be part of your ancient ancestors' recognition of the wheel of life, and be waiting to share the wisdom and understandings which led them to be placed there with any who are willing to listen.

But where do you stand? The answer to this question will not necessarily be the centre, for there lies the point of total balance and harmony, the place where all powers meet and become one, the unity and the stillness. You will almost certainly find that each time you attempt to work from the centre of your circle you become aware of an imbalance and find yourself pulled off centre in order to work with another aspect of yourself. This is how it should be. This is why we are in these bodies living on the Earth at this time. We are working towards balance and harmony, but we have not yet achieved it. Although all of us will have moments of stillness and peace in our lives when we experience the perfection of the centre, these will be to remind us of our purpose and assure us of its ultimate attainability.

Eventually it will become clear that the centre is not one single point, but is in actual fact the entire circle in perfect balance, harmony and unity. This is the goal towards which we all ultimately must work. We are seeking not only the perfection of our own circles, but through them the perfection of the greater circles of which we are a part.

CONCLUSION

When journeying to seek confirmation of information contained within *The Serpent and the Circle* I received the following message.

'Yes, but things are not how you think. Things are far, far beyond mind. What you perceive as the entire ladder is in truth but the bottom rung.'

I apologise that I can at present travel no further with you. It seems that we have been on a long journey together, yet who can measure the distance we have travelled when the paths we have taken are known only to ourselves? What lies ahead is truly awe-inspiring and, perhaps, at times a little frightening.

What has been achieved? In the past a shaman would guide his or her apprentices through experiences that would open within them the channels through which their own learning and development could take place. These channels were not designed to connect them to any external source of wisdom or power, but rather to link together every level within them, so they could initially become as complete, fully realised and harmonious as was possible for them. Once this was achieved they were linked to the part of themselves that knew how to heal and help, not only the people around them, but also every level of being with which they came into contact.

The old ways are no longer with us, nor is it appropriate that they should be. This book has come to you in the stead of an earthly teacher to whom you may once have needed to apprentice a significant part of your life. Simply by reading it the channels within you will have begun to clear. This is regardless of what reaction or opinion your mind may have come up with, which to a large extent will be a conditioned reaction from your education. If you have chosen to work through the book it will change your life. It is as simple as that. Once the channels are open it will be a difficult task for anyone to close them again.

I can give no guarantees about what you will find within yourself. I can promise, however, that when you need help it will be there for you. All you will have to do is recognise and accept it. As we have all experienced, change, albeit for the better, can be painful. And as the channels within you begin to clear you will certainly find yourself involved in a lot of change.

Yet, where do you go from here? Continue to work with the Serpent, walking the spiral path to maintain the balance and harmony that is necessary for your own health and growth. Feel your circle and through that you are connected and can reach out in confidence to the myriads of other circles that join yours.

Some of the most obvious links and connections between the myths, legends, symbology and spiritual traditions of all cultures will now be clear to you. There is so much more to learn and understand, but do not neglect the richest source of myth and symbology that is available to you, which is of course your own. One could search for ever among the many diverse sources of wisdom and learning and never find that which is relevant and meaningful to you. There is a part of you which knows precisely who you are, where you're going and what path you need to take to get there. Let your first aim be consciously to unite with this part of yourself, trusting it above your mind, above your emotions and your physical appetites. Once you truly become yourself you will have found the source of all the myths and esoteric learning in the world, and will be able to study it from its source rather than trying to gather the scattered fragments that are in the world today and make some sense of them.

This is the final task and greatest quest I lay before you. Become the vast being that you truly are – wake up and become yourself!

Resources

Further Reading

Bates, Brian (1986) *The Way of Wyrd*, Arrow Books

Blofeld, John (trans) (1965) *I Ching*, Mandala Books

Boissiere, Robert (1990) *The Return of Pahana*, Bear and Co.

Bruchac, Joseph (1991) *Native American Stories*, Fulcrum Publishing

Bryant, Page (1991) *The Aquarian Guide to Native American Mythology*, Aquarian Press

Colum, Padraic (1986) *The King of Ireland's Son*, Floris Books

Cowan, James (1991) *Letters From A Wild State*, Element Books

Cowan, James (1992) *The Aborigine Tradition*, Element Books

Davidson, John (1987) *Subtle Energy*, C. W. Daniel Co. Ltd

Donner, Florinda (1984) *Shabono*, Triad/Paladin Books

Feldmann, Susan (1965) *The Storytelling Stone: Myths and Tales of the American Indians*, Dell Publishing Co. Inc.

Gidley, M (1979) *With One Sky Above Us*, Windward

Green, Roger Lancelyn (1970) *Myths of the Norsemen*, Puffin Books

Hamel, Peter Michael (1978) *Through Music to the Self*, Element Books

Harner, Michael (1982) *The Way of the Shaman*, Bantam Books

Jung, C. G. (1983) *Memories, Dreams, Reflections*, Flamingo

King, Serge Kahili (1990) *Urban Shaman*, Fireside

Lucas, Penelope (1992) *Wilderness Moon*, Corgi Books

Meadows, Kenneth (1989) *Earth Medicine*, Element Books

Meadows, Kenneth (1990) *The Medicine Way*, Element Books

Meadows, Kenneth (1991) *Shamanic Experience*, Element Books

Neihardt, John G. (1974) *Black Elk Speaks*, Hutchinson

Ozaniec, Naomi (1991) *The Chakras*, Element Books

Pennick, Nigel (1989) *Practical Magic in the Northern Tradition*, Aquarian Press

Rael, Joseph E. (1992) *Beautiful Painted Arrow*, Element Books

Storm, Hyemeyohsts (1972) *Seven Arrows*, Ballantine Books

Walsh, Roger N. (1990) *The Spirit of Shamanism*, Mandala

Young, Ella (1985) *Celtic Wonder Tales*, Floris Books

Zukav, Gary (1990) *The Seat of the Soul*, Rider

Drumming Tape

A drumming tape for shamanic journeys, produced by Kenneth Meadows, is available from Peridot Publishing, 27 Old Gloucester Street, London WC1N 3XX, priced £9.50 including postage and packing.

Contact Address

For information about workshops run by the author please write to:

Namua Rahesha
c/o The Amethyst Centre
The Old Chapel
Chapel Street
Robin Hood's Bay
Whitby
North Yorkshire

Index